HIEROGLYPHIC TEXTS
FROM
EGYPTIAN STELAE

ETC.

THE BRITISH MUSEUM

HIEROGLYPHIC TEXTS FROM EGYPTIAN STELAE ETC.

PART 12

EDITED BY

M. L. BIERBRIER

ASSISTANT KEEPER IN THE DEPARTMENT OF
EGYPTIAN ANTIQUITIES

WITH DRAWINGS BY

RICHARD PARKINSON

PUBLISHED FOR
THE TRUSTEES OF THE BRITISH MUSEUM
BY BRITISH MUSEUM PRESS
1993

Published by British Museum Press
A division of British Museum Publications Ltd
46 Bloomsbury Street, London WC1B 3QQ

Set in Monotype Photina by Southern Positives and Negatives (SPAN), Lingfield, Surrey

Printed in Great Britain by Henry Ling Ltd, Dorchester, Dorset

British Library Cataloguing in Publication Data
A catalogue record for this book is available from the British Library

ISBN 0-7141-0947-9

Preface

Part 12 of the British Museum's *Hieroglyphic Texts* series is devoted to a further selection of inscribed objects dating to the New Kingdom, in this case almost entirely to the Ramesside Period. The material, amounting to nearly eighty individual pieces and of mixed provenance, consists mostly of stelae but also includes architectural pieces, foundation deposits, naoi, statues, a head-rest, a monumental scarab and various other fragments. Each is published in photograph with accompanying line-drawing(s). It should be noted that this volume brings to completion the publication of those hieroglyphic inscriptions in the collection known to have come from the site of Deir el-Medina.

The descriptions and commentaries are the work of Dr Morris Bierbrier, who is an Assistant Keeper in the Department of Egyptian Antiquities. Dr Richard Parkinson, who is a curator in the same department, is responsible for the drawings. The photographic work was carried out by Peter Hayman of the Museum's Photographic Service. Christine Barratt, the Egyptian Department's Graphics Officer, helped prepare the plates for publication. Progress of the volume through press was overseen by Sarah Derry of British Museum Press.

Keeper of Egyptian Antiquities
British Museum
1993

W. V. DAVIES

Abbreviations

Belmore Collection	*Tablets and other Egyptian Monuments from the Collection of the Earl of Belmore now deposited in the British Museum*, 1843.
Bierbrier, *Late New Kingdom*	M. L. Bierbrier, *The Late New Kingdom in Egypt*. Warminster, 1975.
BIFAO	*Bulletin de l'Institut français d'archéologie orientale.*
Bi. Or.	*Bibliotheca Orientalis.*
BMQ	*British Museum Quarterly.*
Bruyère, *Deir el Médineh*	B. Bruyère, *Rapport sur les fouilles de Deir el Médineh*. Cairo, 1924–53.
Bruyère, *Mert Seger*	B. Bruyère, *Mert Seger à Deir el Médineh*. Cairo, 1930.
Černý, *Community*	J. Černý, *A Community of Workmen at Thebes in the Ramesside Period*. Cairo, 1973.
Chron. d'Ég.	*Chronique d'Égypte.*
Guide (1904)	*British Museum. A Guide to the Third and Fourth Egyptian Rooms*. London, 1904.
Guide (1922)	*British Museum. A Guide to the Fourth, Fifth and Sixth Rooms, and the Coptic Room*. London, 1922.
Guide (1930)	*British Museum. A General Introductory Guide to the Egyptian Collections in the British Museum*. London, 1930.
Helck, *Materialien*	W. Helck, *Materialien zur Wirtschaftgeschichte des Neuen Reiches*. Wiesbaden, 1961–69.
HT	The British Museum. *Hieroglyphic Texts from Egyptian Stelae etc.* Vols. 6–11. London, 1922–87.
JARCE	*Journal of the American Research Center in Egypt*, Boston.
JEA	*Journal of Egyptian Archaeology.*
KRI	K. A. Kitchen, *Ramesside Inscriptions*. 8 vols. Oxford, 1968–90.
LÄ	Wolfgang Helck and Eberhard Otto, *Lexikon der Ägyptologie*, Vols. I–VII, 1975–92.
LdR	Henri Gauthier, *Le Livre des rois d'Égypte*, 5 vols. MIFAO 17–21, 1907–17.
Lieblein, *Dictionnaire*	J. Lieblein, *Dictionnaire de noms hiéroglyphiques en ordre généalogique et alphabétique*. Leipzig, 1871–92.
MDAIK	*Mitteilungen des Deutschen Archäologischen Instituts Abteilung Kairo.*
O. Cairo	J. Černý, *Ostraca hiératiques* (Catalogue général des Antiquités égyptiennes du Musée du Caire). Cairo, 1935. Nos. 25501–25832.
Porter and Moss, *Top. Bibl.*	B. Porter and R. L. B. Moss, *Topographical Bibliography of Ancient Egyptian Hieroglyphic Texts, Reliefs and Paintings*. 7 vols. Oxford, 1927–51. Vols. I–III revised 1960–81.
Rec. trav.	*Recueil de travaux relatifs à la philologie et à l'archéologie égyptiennes et assyriennes.*
Rev. d'Ég.	*Revue d'Égyptologie.*
Sculpture Guide (1909)	*British Museum. A Guide to the Egyptian Galleries (Sculpture)*. London, 1909.
Sharpe, *Eg. Inscr.*	S. Sharpe, *Egyptian Inscriptions from the British Museum and other sources*. London, 1837–55.
Spiegelberg, *Graffiti*	W. Spiegelberg, *Ägyptische und andere Graffiti aus der thebanischen Nekropolis*. Heidelberg, 1921.
Synopsis (1848)	*British Museum. Synopsis of the Contents of the British Museum*. London, 1848.
Vandier, *Manuel*	J. Vandier, *Manuel d'archéologie égyptienne*. Vol. III. Paris, 1958.
ZÄS	*Zeitschrift für ägyptische Sprache und Altertumskunde.*

Description of the Plates

Plate 1

Fragments with the name and titulary of Horemheb — 58468b, 58468d

Date: Late Eighteenth Dynasty
Provenance: El-Amarna
Date of acquisition: 1927
Material: Limestone
Dimensions: 9.5 cm *h.*, 10 cm *l.*, 5 cm *deep* (58468b); 12.5 cm *h.*, 28 cm *l.* (58468d)

Two fragments of coarse limestone with parts of the name and titulary of Horemheb with epithets. Fragment 58468b is incised on two faces and reads *nbty | wr biꜣt . . .* Fragment 58468d curves slightly towards the left end and there are remains of a sculpted feature on the top, probably the tail of a sphinx. The inscription reads *mr.f nb ḫꜥw ... sꜣ Rꜥ Ḥr-[m-ḥb] mry-'Imn ...* For similar fragments see *HT* 10, pl. 1, where these two are mentioned as unlocated at that time. The original excavation numbers on the pieces are worn, but that on 58468d appears to read 26–7/S 116.

Preservation and colour: The fragments are broken and worn with the surfaces much damaged. There are traces of blue paint in the hieroglyphs of 58468b. The inscription of 58468d is substantially damaged, and this destruction may well be deliberate.

Bibliography: J. Pendlebury, *City of Akhenaten* III (London, 1951), 12, nos. 26/S 30, 114–17.

Plates 2–3

Statue Base of Sety I — 32623

Date: Nineteenth Dynasty
Provenance: Not recorded
Date of acquisition: 1900
Material: Crystalline limestone
Dimensions: 7.2 cm *h.*, 20.8 cm *w.*, 16.7 cm *deep.*

This fragmentary base is incised on its three surviving sides with a text consisting of the names and epithets of Sety I. The base has been polished on the sides, but on the top only a small area near the edge, varying from 2 cm on the right to 4.5 cm on the left, has been so treated. The rest of the top and the entire bottom of the base are left rough. One circular hole, 2 cm in diameter and made with a tubular drill to a depth of 3.6 cm, is visible on the top, but the remains of two other holes to depths of 3.7 and 4.5 cm are partly preserved along the edge of the break. These were presumably used to attach a statue to the base.

Preservation and colour: Only one part of the entire base has been preserved. This is in good condition apart from a few gouges near the edges. There are traces of blue paint in some of the hieroglyphs.

Bibliography: None.

Plates 4–7

Statue of Ramesses II — 697

Date: Nineteenth Dynasty
Provenance: Serabit el-Khadim
Date of acquisition: 1905[1]
Material: Sandstone
Dimensions: 61.5 cm *h.*, 35.3 cm *w.*, 50.5 cm *deep* (statue); 26.7 cm *h.*, 11.5 cm *w.* (fragment A); 10.4 cm *h.*, 5.5 cm *w.*, 11.8 cm *deep* (fragment B)

The lower half of a standing statue of Ramesses II holding a standard. The statue base is itself on a smaller plinth. The prenomen and nomen of Ramesses II and epithets are incised on the king's skirt (A), the base of the statue (B), the standard (C), the back pillar (D) and along the sides of the base (E and F) together with the names of Hathor, lady of turquoise (E), and Thoth, lord of Punt (F), who are also named on the top of the base (B). On the left side of the statue behind the standard, the figure of Queen Bintanat is carved in sunk relief. Her name is wrongly written 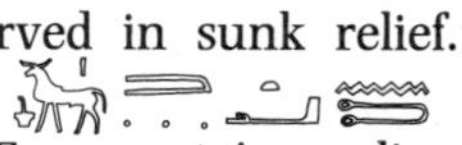 instead of  (G). Fragment A supplies the head for the figure of the queen and part of the back pillar. Fragment B is a portion of the standard with part of the prenomen and epithets.

Bintanat was the daughter of Ramesses II and Queen Isitnofret and was the king's eldest daughter. She is known from several monuments (Gauthier, *LdR* III, 102–3). Like her half-sister Merytamun (for whom see BM 1662 in *HT* 10, pl. 17), she was raised to the rank of queen possibly on the death of her mother. She was buried in Tomb 71 in the Valley of the Queens (Porter and Moss, *Top. Bibl.* I^2, ii, 766–7).

Preservation and colour: The lower half of the statue is well preserved apart from some minor cracks on the base. The upper cartouche on the skirt is damaged. The upper half of the statue is lost with the exception of fragment A which is now joined to the lower half and fragment B. There are no traces of colour.

Bibliography: W. F. Petrie, *Researches in Sinai* (London, 1906), 128–9, pls. 136–7; *Sculpture Guide* (1909), 162 (no. 587); A. H. Gardiner and T. E. Peet, *The Inscriptions of Sinai* I^2 (London, 1952), no. 263, pl. LXXII; II (London, 1955), 181 no. 263; Porter and Moss, *Top. Bibl.* VII, 357; J. Vandier, *Rev. d'Ég.* 16 (1964), 82; *KRI* II, 401–2.

1. Presented by the Egypt Exploration Fund.

Plates 8–9

Foundation deposit brick of Ramesses II — 49234

Date: Nineteenth Dynasty
Provenance: Not recorded
Date of acquisition: 1910
Material: Faience
Dimensions: 6.8 cm *h.*, 17.6 cm *w.*, 36 cm *l.*

The prenomen and nomen of Ramesses II are painted in

black on both surfaces of this brick (A and B). The Horus name, prenomen and nomen of the same king are written in two texts along three sides of the brick (C and D). The text on the fourth side of the brick is now illegible (E), but it probably contained the prenomen and nomen of the king with epithets as in the three comparable bricks discussed below.

This brick was presumably from a foundation deposit and was acquired in Cairo together with BM 49235 (*HT* 10, pl. 22) which comes from Memphis. Memphis might be the provenance of this piece. However, three nearly identical bricks are known, one in the Metropolitan Museum of New York (W. C. Hayes, *Glazed Tiles from a Palace of Ramesses II at Kantir* (New York, 1937, 6), another formerly in the MacGregor collection (H. Wallis, *Egyptian Ceramic Art* (London, 1898), 30; Lot 1324 in the *Catalogue of the MacGregor Collection of Egyptian Antiquities*, Sotheby, 26 June 1922), and a third which is unpublished in the Freer Art Gallery, Washington (09.147). Hayes argues that the bricks originate from Qantir, but as none was discovered *in situ*, the question of provenance remains unresolved. The Freer brick was acquired in 1909 from the same Cairo dealer (M. Nahman) as EA 49234 so there can be little doubt that these two come from the same provenance.

Preservation and colour: The brick is chipped at two corners and badly worn along two sides which are now largely illegible. The faience is light green.

Bibliography: None.

Plates 10–11

Statue base of Ramesses II 29282

Date: Nineteenth Dynasty
Provenance: Not recorded
Date of acquisition: 1897
Material: Sandstone and alabaster
Dimensions: 11.5 cm *h.*, 33 cm *l.*, 13.5 cm *w.*, (base); 3.5 cm *h.*, 19.2 cm *l.*, 8.3 cm *w.* (statue)

This small sandstone statue base is inscribed on all sides: front (A), right (B), left (C), back (D) and top (E). The inscriptions consist of the prenomen and nomen of Ramesses II with epithets. On the top of the base stood an alabaster statue of Ramesses II striding over the nine bows which are incised on the top of the base.

Preservation and colour: Only the feet of the original statue remain firmly fixed in place on the top of the base. The base itself is worn along the edges and corners but is otherwise well preserved.

Bibliography: None.

Plates 12–13

1. Scarab of Ramesses II 1231

Date: Nineteenth Dynasty
Provenance: Not recorded
Date of acquisition: 1897
Material: Grey granite
Dimensions: 29.3 cm *h.*, 39 cm *w.*, 54 cm *l.*

This scarab is inscribed on one side with the names of Ramesses II and epithets. The other sides are now rough and show signs of deliberate erasure. It is difficult to determine whether the surviving inscription was recut on a repolished surface as this surface is not deeply indented. However, this seems more likely than a subsequent erasure of part of the inscription of Ramesses II.

Preservation and colour: The monument is badly worn in many places. The corners are damaged, and there are many gouges on the surface.

Bibliography: British Museum, *Please Touch Animal Sculpture* (London, 1983), no. 13.

2. Stela of Ramesses II 68675

Date: Nineteenth Dynasty
Provenance: Amara West
Date of acquisition: 1976[1]
Material: Sandstone
Dimensions: 50 cm *h.*, 34 cm *w.*

This crudely carved stela depicts Ramesses II on the right, offering ointment jars to the goddess Satet on the left. Between them is an altar on which rests a water-pot cooled by a lotus flower.

Preservation and colour: The stela is badly worn with loss to some of the incised texts.

Bibliography: Porter and Moss, *Top. Bibl.* VII, 163; D. Valbelle, *Satis et Anoukis*, 1981, 43, no. 325; V. W. Davies, *Egypt and Africa*, 1991, 316, pl. 14.

1. Presented by the Egypt Exploration Society.

Plates 14–15

1. Foundation deposits of Tausret 29951, 29952

Date: Nineteenth Dynasty
Provenance: Not recorded
Date of acquisition: 1898
Material: Sandstone
Dimensions: 17.5 cm *w.*, 30.5 cm *l.*, 6.5 cm *thick* (29951); 16.3 cm *w.*, 29.5 cm *l.*, 6.5 cm *thick* (29952)

There can be no doubt that these two bricks, deeply carved on one side with the prenomen and nomen of Tausret, came from her mortuary temple at Thebes excavated by Petrie in 1896 (Petrie, *Six Temples at Thebes* (London, 1897), 13–16 and pl. XVII (2); Porter and Moss, *Top. Bibl.* II², 447; *KRI* IV, 353). Another example is in the Petrie Museum, UCL 14377 (H. Stewart, *Egyptian Stelae, Reliefs and Paintings from the Petrie Collection* (Warminster, 1976), 7, pl. 4, no. 5).

Preservation and colour: Apart from slight chipping on the edges, the bricks are well preserved. There are no traces of colour.

Bibliography: *Guide* (1922), 136 (no. 7).

2. Foundation deposit of Ramesses IV (?) 54420

Date: Twentieth Dynasty
Provenance: Not recorded
Date of acquisition: 1919
Material: Faience
Dimensions: 9.5 cm *h.*, 5.5 cm *w.*

The prenomen and nomen of a Ramesses are incised on

one side of this plaque, while the other side bears an incised decoration, perhaps of part of a temple. It is possible that the badly written royal name is that of *Wsr-<mꜣ^ct>-r^c stp-n-'Imn R^cmssw mry-'Imn*, i.e. Ramesses IV in his first year. This piece was acquired in Luxor and may have come from one of the temples of Ramesses IV in that area.

Preservation and colour: The blue faience plaque is much faded. The incised signs are inlaid with black glaze.

Bibliography: *Guide* (1922), 214 (no. 49); *KRI* VII, 326.

3. Fragment of Ramesses VI 68173

Date: Twentieth Dynasty
Provenance: Saqqara
Date of acquisition: 1971[1]
Material: Wood
Dimensions: 35 cm *h.*, 5.5 cm *w.*

This wooden fragment is incised with the Horus name *kꜣ nḫt ꜥꜣ nḫt* ... The only pharaoh whose Horus name fits these traces is Ramesses VI, whose Horus name was *kꜣ nḫt ꜥꜣ nḫtw sꜥnḫ tꜣwy* (Gauthier, *LdR* III, 197–200). This fragment probably belonged to a shrine.

Preservation and colour: This fragment is covered in slight cracks, and there are several large gouges on the surface. There are no traces of colour.

Bibliography: None.

1. Presented by the Egypt Exploration Society.

Plates 16–17

Stela of the viceroy *Ḥri* 1784

Date: Twentieth Dynasty
Provenance: Amara West
Date of acquisition: 1939[1]
Material: Sandstone
Dimensions: 130 cm *h.*, 71 cm *w.*

This large, round-topped stela is divided into two distinct sections with figures in sunk relief and incised texts. At the top Ramesses III stands on the right, offering to Amen-Reꜥ, a goddess, presumably Bastet,[2] and Horus. Three lines of text give the date of year 11 and the full titulary of the king. The lower section of the stela consists of four columns of text on the right containing a prayer by the viceroy of Kush Hori. The viceroy and his deputy kneel in adoration on the left. Below, a single line of text names the deputy *Pꜣ-sr*, son of *P(ꜣ)-n-rꜥ*.

The viceroy of Kush Hori, son of Hori son of Kama, is well attested. He was in office from at least year 5 of Ramesses III until the reign of Ramesses IV (*KRI* V, 381–3; VI, 79–81).

Preservation and colour: The stela is heavily worn, and much of the surface has been lost, especially at the top.

Bibliography: H. Fairman, *JEA* 25 (1939), 143; H. Fairman, *The Connoisseur* 103 (1939), 327; Porter and Moss, *Top. Bibl.* VII, 162; *KRI* V, 382–3.

1. Presented by the Egypt Exploration Fund.
2. Compare Khartoum Museum 3061 from Amara West with the same triad (*JEA* 25 (1939), pl. xv, no. 2).

Plates 18–19

Stela of the viceroy *Ḥri* 66668

Date: Twentieth Dynasty
Provenance: Buhen
Date of acquisition: 1964[1]
Material: Sandstone
Dimensions: 163 cm *h.*, 115 cm *w.*

This large stela was made in the form of a doorway with a cavetto-cornice and torus-moulding at the top on which is incised a winged sun disk. The lintel and jambs are incised with the full titulary of Ramesses IV. The main stela is divided into two principal sections. At the top the king on the left offers Maat to Horus, Lord of Buhen, who flourishes a *hpš*-sword, Isis and Bastet. Six lines of text contain a prayer for Ramesses IV. In the lower register the king's cartouches are carved on the right, while on the left the viceroy kneels in adoration. Before him are four columns of text with a hymn to the king by the viceroy of Kush Hori, son of Hori, son of *Kmꜥ*.

For Hori see BM 1784 above.

Preservation and colour: The stela has been broken into several fragments which have been joined together, but parts of the centre, upper left and top are lost. The surviving pieces are worn in places, especially the upper right jamb. There are no traces of colour.

Bibliography: *BMQ* 29 (1964–5), 125 (no. 3); H. Smith, *The Fortress of Buhen: The Inscriptions* (London, 1976), 151–3, pl. 79; *KRI* VI, 80–1.

1. Presented by the Egypt Exploration Society.

Plates 20–21

1. Lintel of the viceroy *Ḥri* 66667

Date: Twentieth Dynasty
Provenance: Buhen
Date of acquisition: 1964[1]
Material: Sandstone
Dimensions: 54.5 cm *h.*, 95.5 cm *l.*

This fragment of a large lintel consists of the torus roll and cornice with incised scenes and texts. A portion of the right side of the lintel was discovered separately and is now unlocated (H. Smith, *The Fortress of Buhen: The Inscriptions* (London, 1976), 118–19, no. 1511, pls. XXV/1, LXXIV/2–3). In the centre of the lintel are the cartouches of Ramesses III. On the left side the viceroy of Kush Hori and the mayor of Buhen *Ḥr-ms* kneel in adoration. Several columns of text are inscribed with a prayer to the king on their behalf. A similar scene was incised on the now lost right-hand portion of the lintel, possibly in the Khartoum Museum.

The viceroy Hori can be identified either with Hori, son of Kama, who is last attested under Sethnakhte (*KRI* V, 2) or, more likely, his son Hori, who was in office from at least year 5 of Ramesses III until the end of the reign (*KRI* V, 381–3).

Preservation and colour: The lintel is battered about the edges, with the loss of the upper left corner and the right side which was recovered separately. The surface is worn in places so that the text is difficult to interpret. There are no traces of colour.

Bibliography: *Orientalia* 33 (1964), 375; A. F. Shore, *BMQ* 29

(1964–5), 125; Smith, *op. cit.*, 118–19, no. 1511, pls. XXV/1, LXXIV/2–3; *KRI* V, 381.

1. Presented by the Egypt Exploration Society.

2. Relief of *'Imn-ms* 1654

Date: Nineteenth Dynasty
Provenance: Abydos
Date of acquisition: 1926[1]
Material: Limestone
Dimensions: 35.8 cm *h.*, 95 cm *l.*

This relief is divided into two scenes carved in sunk relief with incised texts. On the left the charioteer Amenmose and his son, the scribe *Mḥw*, adore Osiris and the four sons of Horus who stand in mummiform guise on a lotus blossom in front of Osiris. On the right side of the relief the scribe of the treasury Mahu, and his mother, the chantress of Amun *Ḥwt.ḥr*, adore the god Anubis who stands behind an altar on which rests a water-pot cooled by a lotus blossom.

Amenmose can be identified with the charioteer of the lord of the two lands, Amenmose, who appears together with his wife, the chantress of Horus the Behdetite Hathor, on the stela of their son, the scribe of the treasury of the temple of Ramesses-meryamun in the estate of Re[c] Mahu, now in the Turin Museum (J. Ruffle, *Glimpses of Ancient Egypt* (Warminster, 1979), 56, 63 pl. III; *KRI* III, 444–5). The appearance of the steward of the Ramesseum Yupa on the Turin stela dates it to the reign of Ramesses II.

Bibliography: H. Frankfort, *JEA* 14 (1928), 243, No. 13, pl. 23:3; Porter and Moss, *Top. Bibl.* V, 65; *KRI* III, 248–9.

1. Presented by the Egypt Exploration Society.

Plates 22–23

1. Stela of *'Imn-ms* 142

Date: Nineteenth Dynasty
Provenance: Not recorded[1]
Date of acquisition: 1834 (Sams collection)
Material: Limestone
Dimensions: 58.2 cm *h.*, 78 cm *w.*

This large fragment consists of the lower part of a stela or relief with eleven lines of incised text naming the royal table-scribe of the lord of the two lands, overseer of huntsmen of Amun, and steward of the temple of Ramesses-meryamun-*ᶜn-ẖr-ḥb-sd-mryt-mi-'Imn*, Amenmose, son of the great carpenter (?) of the lord of the two lands *Rᶜ-ms*, and the chantress of Amun *Nfrt-iry*.

Amenmose is known from his unpublished tomb 149 at Thebes (Porter and Moss, *Top. Bibl.* I², i, 260) where the name of his wife Sitmut also apparently appears. A further fragment of his is also in the British Museum (BM 107). The temple in which he served is otherwise unknown (Helck, *Materialien*, 57).

Preservation and colour: The surviving portion of this stela is well preserved apart from a number of gouges on the surface of the stone and damage along the edges, especially at the top.

Bibliography: *Synopsis* (1848), 160 (no. 142); *Sculpture Guide* (1909), 202 (no. 735); *KRI* III, 218–19.

1. The provenance of Thebes given in 1909 is not based on any external evidence but is probably correct.

2. Stela of *'Imn-ms* 107

Date: Nineteenth Dynasty
Provenance: Not recorded
Date of acquisition: Not recorded
Material: Limestone
Dimensions: 46.3 cm *h.*, 37.7 cm *w.*

This rectangular piece has been cut from the left side of a stela. The edge of a round-topped stela is incised on the left side. At the top three worshippers stand in adoration of an object, possibly a standard, which is largely destroyed. Several columns of text incised above and beside the figures gave their names, mostly now lost. The figures are a small girl, a man and a woman, the chantress of Amun *Nfrt-iry*. Below the scene are the remains of four lines of text, the first of which names [the table-scribe] of the lord of the two lands and chief huntsman of Amun, Amenmose. On the reverse of this fragment, at a ninety-degree angle to the inscription on the other side, are three lines of text which again name the table-scribe of the lord of the two lands, [Amen]mose, son of *Rᶜ-ms*.

For Amenmose see BM 142 above. The lady Nefertari can be identified as his mother, but the young girl remains unidentified and is possibly a daughter. This piece may also have come from his tomb 149 at Thebes.

Preservation and colour: This piece is in a poor state of preservation. It has been extensively damaged with much loss to the right side of the obverse and most of the reverse. Salt damage has resulted in some loss since the original photographs used here were taken.

Bibliography: *Sculpture Guide* (1909), 188 (no. 677).

Plates 24–25

1. Bust of *Mwt-m-int* 1198

Date: Nineteenth Dynasty
Provenance: Not recorded[1]
Date of acquisition: 1897
Material: Limestone
Dimensions: 49 cm *h.*, 19 cm *w.*

This finely carved bust is incised with three columns of text. The main text bears a dedication to the sistrum-player of Amun, Mut, and Khons, Mutemonet.[2] The back is roughly finished.

A parallel bust of Pendjerti, husband of Mutemonet, has been discovered in the tomb of their son Amenmose, no. 373 at Thebes. There can be no doubt that this bust was one of a pair from that tomb. The royal scribe Amenmose is attested on several monuments and flourished in the reign of Rameses II (L. Habachi in *Studies in Honor of George R. Hughes* (Chicago, 1976), 83–103; *KRI* III, 213–18).

Preservation and colour: The bust has been severely damaged at the base and back with much loss of the stone surface. There are a few gouges on the body and face. There are slight traces of black in the *in* hieroglyph in the central column of the text.

Bibliography: *Sculpture Guide* (1909), 238 (no. 871); L. Habachi in *Studies in Honor of George R. Hughes* (Chicago, 1976), 85–6; *The Luxor Museum of Ancient Art Catalogue* (Cairo, 1979), 150; *KRI* III, 216.

1. Undoubtedly Thebes, Tomb 373.
2. Her title is uncertain. If it is to be read *iḥyt*, then this is its earliest occurrence. However, this may be a rare spelling of *šmᶜyt* or even *sššyt*.

Plates 24–27

2. Statue of *Ḥꜣti* 1726

Date: Nineteenth–Twentieth Dynasty
Provenance: Not recorded
Date of acquisition: 1930
Material: Limestone
Dimensions: 41 cm *h.*, 25.5 cm *w.*, 29.5 cm *deep*

A block statue squatting on a cushion with figures of Onuris-Shu and Mehit in front of it. The name of the owner, the temple-scribe of Onuris Hati, is incised twice on the top of the statue (A). The names of Onuris-Shu and Mehit and a brief prayer appear on the front of the statue (B). Four horizontal lines of text containing a prayer to Onuris, Horus lord of Thinis and Meh[it] on behalf of Hati are incised on the right side of the statue (C). A similar inscription, much broken, appears on the left side of the statue (D). The name and titles of Hati are also incised on the back pillar (E).

The titles of Hati would appear to indicate that he held office in the temple of Onuris at Thinis, probably the site of Nag el-Mashayikh (Porter and Moss, *Top. Bibl.* V, 28–9). A temple of Ramesses III is attested there (Helck, *Materialien*, 169), and one of Hati's titles indicates that there was a construction of Ramesses II at Thinis as well. This statue may have come from Thinis or possibly Abydos where objects bearing references to Thinis have been found (Porter and Moss, *Top. Bibl.* V, 67–8, 74).

Preservation and colour: This statue is in an extremely poor state of preservation and has suffered much damage both before and after its acquisition. The head is now almost lost, and the figure of Mehit and the accompanying inscription have undergone further deterioration since the statue was initially photographed. The drawing of the front on pl. 27 is taken from the earlier photograph. The statue is severely cracked along both sides with loss to the inscriptions and has been repaired in modern times. The lower back pillar is also damaged.

Bibliography: *BMQ* 5, 19.

Plates 28–29

1. Wooden fragment of *Nfr-ᶜbw* 65593

Date: Nineteenth Dynasty
Provenance: Not recorded[1]
Date of acquisition: 1955[2]
Material: Wood
Dimensions: 41 cm *h.*, 14.5 cm *w.*

This wooden fragment is covered in linen to which a thin layer of plaster has been applied. Six columns of text are painted on the plaster and contain a hymn to Reᶜ-Harakhty-Atum by the workman Neferᶜabu.

Neferᶜabu is a well-known workman at Deir el-Medina, flourishing in the early part of the reign of Ramesses II (*HT* 9, pl. 30; J. Vandier, *La Tombe de Nefer-abou* (Cairo, 1935); *KRI* III, 521, 766–80). This fragment probably belongs to an object from Neferᶜabu's funerary equipment and so may derive from his tomb, no. 5 at Deir el-Medina.

Preservation and colour: Only a fragment of the original object survives. The edges are worn and chipped with loss of text. No column is completely preserved, and only the edges of the sixth column remain. The background of the text is painted white, while the text itself is painted in black with red dividing lines between the columns. Traces of the original red draft of the text are visible. The border at the top is painted dark green with traces of blue above. The underside of the fragment is not plastered.

Bibliography: Porter and Moss, *Top. Bibl.* I^2, ii, 14; *KRI* III, 778.

1. Undoubtedly Deir el-Medina on internal evidence.
2. Presented by J. H. M. Wright.

2. Figure of Meresger dedicated by *Nfr-ᶜbw* 2559

Date: Nineteenth Dynasty
Provenance: Not recorded[1]
Date of acquisition: 1843 (Belmore collection)
Material: Wood
Dimensions: 59.7 cm *h.*, 7.5 cm *w.* (at top of pedestal), 10.5 cm *w.* (at shoulders)

This fine figure of the goddess Meresger in the form of a human-headed serpent on a pedestal is incised with prayers to Meresger and to Amen-Reᶜ on behalf of Neferᶜabu.

Neferᶜabu, who dedicated this statuette, can be identified with the well-known necropolis-workman Neferᶜabu at Deir el-Medina, for whom see BM 65593 above.

Preservation and colour: The figure is carved only at the front, while the back is undecorated. The back of the pedestal is badly worn and warped. The front of the statue has been painted red-brown. There are several large cracks down the front. There is a hole on the top of the head for an attachment of some other object. The eyes and eyebrows are carved and painted black. There are several incised bands across the front of the figure, and these were filled with blue paint of which traces remain. The nose is slightly damaged.

Bibliography: *Guide* (1904), 278 (no. 6).

1. Undoubtedly Deir el-Medina on internal evidence.

Plates 30–31

1. Stela of *Mꜣꜣ-n.ỉ-nḫt.f* 269

Date: Nineteenth Dynasty
Provenance: Thebes[1]
Date of acquisition: 1843 (Belmore collection)
Material: Limestone
Dimensions: 36.5 cm *h.* (restored); 25.5 cm *w.*

Two scenes are carved in sunk relief on this round-topped stela, and all texts are incised. In the upper register the deceased, whose name is lost, stands in adoration on the right before an altar on which rests a water-pot cooled by lotus blossoms. Behind it the god Ptah is enthroned followed by a standing figure of the goddess Maat. Below, in the lower register, the necropolis-workmen Maaninakhtef and *Nfr-ᶜbw* kneel in worship.

Maaninakhtef and Neferᶜabu are well-known workmen in the early part of the reign of Ramesses II (see BM 65593 above; *HT* 9, pl. 30, 34–5; *KRI* III 650–2; M.-C. Budischovsky and N. Genaille, *Annales de Bretagne et des Pays de l'Ouest* 93 (1986) 9–18). Maaninakhtef was married to the sister of Neferᶜabu (Bierbrier, *JEA* 66 (1980), 104–5). A second joint stela of the brothers-in-law is now in the Musée de Rennes (see Budischovsky and Genaille, *op. cit.*, 9–18).

Preservation and colour: The stela is in a poor state of preservation. It has been broken in two and repaired in modern times. The upper edge and upper right side are lost and have been restored. The bottom edge has also been severely damaged. The surviving surface is much worn. Traces of red paint remain on the bodies of the figures, the outline of Ptah's body, the dress of Maat and the dividing lines between the columns of text. Blue traces can be seen in the hieroglyphs, the line between the two registers, the wig of the first kneeling human figure, the collar and wig of Maat and the cap of Ptah. Ptah's collars are red and black.

Bibliography: *Sculpture Guide* (1909), 149 (no. 537); *HT* 7, pl. 40; Porter and Moss, *Top. Bibl.* I², ii, 725; *KRI* III, 651; Budischovsky and Genaille, *op. cit.*, 9–18.

1. Undoubtedly Deir el-Medina on internal evidence.

2. Stela of *Ḫ^{c}-bḫnt* 555

Date: Nineteenth Dynasty
Provenance: Thebes[1]
Date of acquisition: 1843 (Belmore collection)
Material: Limestone
Dimensions: 63.5 cm *h.*, 41.5 cm *w.*

This round-topped stela is divided into three scenes in sunk relief with incised texts. In the upper register is the bark of Re^{c}-Harakhty with a figure of the god in raised relief in the centre of the disk. On the left is an *udjat*-eye and on the right a *šn* sign. In the middle register the necropolis-workman Khabekhnet kneels in adoration on the left before a royal figure with a sidelock, probably a deified prince, and the goddess Hathor in the form of a cow emerging from a mountain. In the lower register Khabekhnet and his wife *Sꜣḥti* kneel in adoration on the left. There are nine columns of text with a prayer to Hathor on their behalf.

The workman Khabekhnet, son of the workman Sennedjem, and his wife Sahte, daughter of the sculptor Piay, flourished in the early part of the reign of Ramesses II (Bierbrier, *Late New Kingdom*, 30–1; Bierbrier, *JEA* 68 (1982), 85–92; *KRI* III, 799–817).

Preservation and colour: The stela is well preserved apart from some damage around the edges and some wear on the surface. There are traces of yellow paint in the hieroglyphs and on the bark, figures, altar, cow and mountain.

Bibliography: *Belmore Collection*, pl. 21; Maspero, *Rec. trav.* 11 (1880), 189–90; Lieblein, *Dictionnaire* No. 999; *Sculpture Guide* (1909), 174 (no. 630); *Guide* (1930), 200, fig. 108; *HT* 7, pl. 31; Porter and Moss, *Top. Bibl.* I², i, 8; *KRI* III, 816–17.

1. Undoubtedly Deir el-Medina on internal evidence, possibly from Tomb 2 of Khabekhnet.

Plates 32–33

1. Stela of *Pꜣ-šd* 264

Date: Ramesside
Provenance: Not recorded[1]
Date of acquisition: 1843 (Belmore collection)
Material: Limestone
Dimensions: 29.4 cm *h.*, 28.8 cm *w.*

This stela was divided into two sections decorated in sunk relief with incised texts. The upper register, now mostly lost, depicted the god Reshep seated in the centre before an altar piled with offerings on the right. Below, in the second register, are seven columns of text consisting of a prayer to Reshep by the necropolis-workman Pashed who is shown kneeling in adoration on the right.

The name of Pashed is too common in Deir el-Medina for precise identification. However, a workman Pashed and his son Pennub did dedicate a stela to Reshep (J. Janssen, *Chron. d'Ég.* 25 (1950), 207–12; *KRI* IV, 241), and this stela might belong to the same man. For his family see BM 341 below.

Preservation and colour: The stela has been broken across the centre with the consequent loss of most of the upper portion of the stone. The preserved fragment is in good condition with only slight scratches and some discolouration on the surface.

Bibliography: *Sculpture Guide* (1909), 135 (no. 478); *HT* 7, pl. 41; J. Fulco, *The Canaanite God Rešep* (New Haven, 1976), 8 (no. E17); Porter and Moss, *Top. Bibl.* I², ii, 732; *KRI* IV, 241.

1. Undoubtedly Deir el-Medina on internal evidence.

2. Stela of *Pꜣ-šd* 341

Date: Ramesside
Provenance: Not recorded[1]
Date of acquisition: Not recorded
Material: Limestone
Dimensions: 34.5 cm *h.*, 23.5 cm *w.*

The god Amen-Re^{c} is enthroned on the right of this round-topped stela. The necropolis-workman Pashed stands on the left in adoration. Below the figures are two lines of text naming the necropolis-workman *P(ꜣ)-n-nw*(?). The figures are in sunk relief and all texts are incised.

There are many workmen named Pashed in the Deir el-Medina community during the Ramesside period. The name of the workman in the last line appears to be garbled. It is possible that the sign 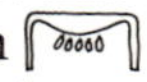 was not completely carved as the area between the two strokes is left blank rather than damaged later. If the name can be read as Pennub, another stela (Fitzwilliam Museum EGA 3002.1943) names a workman Pashed and his son Pennub (J. Janssen, *Chron. d'Ég.* 25 (1950), 207–12; *KRI* IV, 241). This Pashed should be identified with the workman Pashed, son of Pennub, who flourished under Amenmesse (J. Janssen, *Commodity Prices from the Ramesside Period* (Leiden, 1975), 77). His father, Pennub the Elder, is known from an ostracon of year 40 of Ramesses II, while another Pennub who appears at the end of the Nineteenth Dynasty is probably to be identified as Pennub, the younger son of Pashed (Janssen, *op. cit.*, 77).

Preservation and colour: The stela is battered about the edges, and there are several gouges on the surface. The area around the god's head appears to have been damaged and then repaired in antiquity. There are no traces of colour, but there are remains of plaster in some of the hieroglyphs.

Bibliography: *Sculpture Guide* (1909), 129–30 (no. 459); *HT* 7, pl. 25; Porter and Moss, *Top. Bibl.* I², ii, 732; *KRI* IV, 240.

1. Undoubtedly Deir el-Medina.

Plates 34–35

1. Stela of . . . *p3-ḥᶜp* 371

Date: Ramesside
Provenance: Not recorded[1]
Date of acquisition: 1823 (Salt collection)[2]
Material: Limestone
Dimensions: 23.9 cm *h.*, 15.5 cm *w.*

This round-topped stela is divided into two registers. The scenes and inscriptions are indicated in black ink, possibly as preparatory sketches for carving which never took place. In the upper register the workman . . . pahapi kneels on the right in adoration of the goddess Meresger in the form of a snake on the left. In the lower register a male and two females are depicted in an attitude of worship. The texts name his son *Nḫt-'Imn*, his mother, the lady *Nfr-m-mr.s(t)* (?), her daughter *Ḥr.s*, her daughter *Mry*, her daughter *'Ifm*(?), and her daughter *'Ii*.

The family cannot be further identified. A scribe Penpahapi is attested under Merenptah (O. Cairo 25504), while a door-keeper Penpahapi (wrongly read as Penpayom or Penpamer) appears under Ramesses III and IV (Janssen, *Commodity Prices*, 29). A coppersmith Ptahpahapi appears under Ramesses III (Janssen, *op. cit.*, 67), while a later Ptahpahapi, son of Kenherkhepeshef, is attested in the middle of the dynasty (Spiegelberg, *Graffiti* Nos. 803, 860, 868–9). Finally, two Amenpahapis are known from the Twentieth Dynasty, one of whom is definitely not this man (Janssen, *op. cit.*, 43; Bierbrier, *JEA* 66 (1980), 103 and note 29 where the true reading of the last element of the name is established).

Preservation and colour: The text has been painted in black ink, while the figures and dividing lines have been outlined in red and corrected in black ink. The ink has faded badly in some areas. The surface is scratched and there are chips along the edges of the stela, especially in the lower left corner.

Bibliography: T. Young, *Hierglyphics collected by the Egyptian Society* (London, 1823–8), pl. 50; S. Sharpe, *Egyptian Antiquities in the British Museum* (London, 1862), 99, no. 371; *Sculpture Guide* (1909) 150 (no. 540); *HT* 7, pl. 29; Bruyère, *Mert Seger*, fig. 51; Porter and Moss, *Top. Bibl.* I², ii, 731.

1. Undoubtedly Deir el-Medina on internal evidence.
2. Birch and Budge wrongly give the Sams collection, but Young, the earliest source, indicates the Salt collection which must be correct.

2. Stela of *'Imn-m-ipt* 816

Date: Ramesside
Provenance: Not recorded[1]
Date of acquisition: 1854 (Valentia collection)[2]
Material: Limestone
Dimensions: 28.7 cm *h.*, 29.7 cm *w.*

There are two registers on this round-topped stela with incised texts and scenes in sunk relief. In the upper register Amenemope, undoubtedly a necropolis-workman, stands in adoration on the right holding up an offering to Amenresonther, Mut and the deified Amenophis I who are enthroned on the left behind an altar heaped with offerings. The second register is badly damaged with only parts of four columns of text still extant.

The name Amenemope is too common at Deir el-Medina for this workman to be identified precisely (see, for example, M. Bierbrier, *Chron. d'Ég.* 59 (1984), 213–19).

Preservation and colour: Only the upper part of this stela is preserved, and this is severely damaged along the upper edge. There is a thick black line along the edges of the stela possibly due to a mounting in the nineteenth century.

Bibliography: *Sculpture Guide* (1909), 103 (no. 354); *HT* 6, pl. 34; J. Černý, *BIFAO* 27 (1927), 165 fig. 3; Porter and Moss, *Top. Bibl.* I², ii, 715.

1. Undoubtedly Deir el-Medina on internal evidence.
2. Presented by A. Lyttleton Annesley.

Plates 36–37

1. Stela of *'Iry-nfr* 284

Date: Nineteenth Dynasty
Provenance: Thebes[1]
Date of acquisition: 1843 (Belmore collection)
Material: Limestone
Dimensions: 30.5 cm *h.*, 21.5 cm *w.*

There are two registers on this round-topped stela decorated in sunk relief with incised texts. In the upper section the goddess Taweret stands on the left, while on the right lies an altar heaped with offerings. Below, in the second part of the stela, the necropolis-workman Irynefer kneels in adoration together with his wife *Mḥy(t)-ḫᶜ.ti* who carries a brazier of incense.

The workman Irynefer and his wife flourished in the early part of the reign of Ramesses II and are attested in his tomb, no. 290, and several stelae (*KRI* III, 714–20).

Preservation and colour: The stela is well preserved apart from the top left-hand corner which has been lost and restored in modern times. The surface is covered in small scratches, and the edges are worn. Traces of red paint remain on the figure of Taweret, some of the offerings, the human figures and the dress of the lady. There are traces of yellow on the altar and black on the wig of Irynefer.

Bibliography: *Belmore Collection*, pl. 22; S. Sharpe, *Egyptian Antiquities in the British Museum* (London, 1862), 50, no. 284; Maspero, *Rec. trav.* 11 (1880), 171; *Sculpture Guide* (1909), 149–50 (no. 538); *HT* 7, pl. 33; B. Bruyère and C. Kuentz, *La Tombe de Nakht-Min et la tombe d'Ari-Nefer* (Cairo, 1926), 105–6, pl. 20; Porter and Moss, *Top. Bibl.* I², ii, 722; *KRI* III, 718.

1. Undoubtedly Deir el-Medina on internal evidence.

2. Stela of *'Iry-nfr* 814

Date: Nineteenth Dynasty
Provenance: Not recorded[1]
Date of acquisition: 1854 (Valentia collection)[2]
Material: Limestone
Dimensions: 33 cm *h.*, 22 cm *w.*

This round-topped stela is divided into two registers with scenes in sunk relief and incised texts. In the upper section the necropolis-workman Irynefer, with an offering in one hand, kneels in adoration on the right before an altar heaped with offerings. The name of the workman is garbled as the male determinative is placed before the *nefer* sign. On the left is the goddess Hathor in the form of a cow standing in a kiosk on a sledge. Above her is a one-winged sun disk. The two registers are divided by a line of text. Below are eight columns of text with a prayer to Hathor on behalf of Irynefer. He kneels in the bottom right-hand corner in an attitude of adoration.

For the workman Irynefer see BM 284 above.

Preservation and colour: The stela is well preserved apart from an ancient repair which has been inserted into its centre, possibly to replace a nodule of flint or some ancient damage. Several signs terminate at the edge of the repair which might indicate that they were fully carved before the damage and repair. The edges of the stela are battered in places. The upper and lower edges are covered in black paint, probably modern.

Bibliography: Sharpe, *Eg. Inscr.*, 2nd ser., 94; *Sculpture Guide* (1909), 149 (no. 536); *HT* 7, pl. 32; B. Bruyère and C. Kuentz, *La Tombe de Nakht-Min et la tombe d'Ari-Nefer* (Cairo, 1926), 106–7, pl. 20; Porter and Moss, *Top. Bibl.* I^{2}, ii, 722; *KRI* III, 814–15.

1. Undoubtedly Deir el-Medina on internal evidence.
2. Presented by A. Lyttleton Annesley.

Plates 38–39

1. Stela of *Pꜣ-rn-nfr* 1347

Date: Nineteenth Dynasty
Provenance: Not recorded[1]
Date of acquisition: 1901
Material: Limestone
Dimensions: 59 cm *h.*, 45.5 cm *w.*

This round-topped stela is divided into two registers with incised texts and figures in sunk relief. At the top of the upper register is a winged sun-disk with uraei. The register itself is divided into two scenes. On the right the workman Parennefer makes an offering of a brazier of incense to the deified Queen Ahmes-Nefertari who is enthroned behind an altar heaped with food offerings. In a similar scene on the left Parennefer makes an offering to the deified King Amenhotep I. In the lower register there is an altar heaped with offerings in the centre. Parennefer stands on the left holding a brazier and followed by his son, whose name is lost, and his son *Bꜣk-n-Mwt* who both hold floral bouquets. His wife *Mwt-m-wiꜣ* stands on the right of the altar holding a vase followed by her daughters *Wrnr* and *Šrit-[R^{c}]*, otherwise known as *Tꜣ . . . nbt*, who each hold a lotus blossom in one hand and a vase in the other.

Parennefer appears on two other stelae, BM 271 (see below) and BM 283 (*HT* 9, 52–3, pl. 42) which names his wife Mutemwia, two sons Sety and Bakenmut, and a daughter Werner. It is probable that the name of Sety should be restored as the first son on BM 1347, but, as the stela is badly gouged, it is not certain that this name was deliberately mutilated since its loss may have been coincidental. Apart from these three stelae, Parennefer and his family are otherwise unattested.

Preservation and colour: The surface of this stela is badly gouged, pitted and cracked. There are no traces of colour.

Bibliography: *Sculpture Guide* (1909), 102–3 (no. 353); *HT* 6, pl. 36; J. Černý, *BIFAO* 27 (1927), 165 fig. 165.

1. Undoubtedly Deir el-Medina on internal evidence.

2. Stela of *Pꜣ-rn-nfr* 271

Date: Nineteenth Dynasty
Provenance: Not recorded
Date of acquisition: 1843 (Belmore collection)
Material: Limestone
Dimensions: 25.5 cm *h.*, 21 cm *w.*

There are two sections on this stela whose top is not extant. A solar bark resting on a sky sign is depicted in raised relief in the upper register. Below seven columns of text are incised, consisting of a prayer to Re^{c} on behalf of the necropolis-workman Parennefer who is shown in sunk relief on the right in an attitude of adoration.

For Parennefer see BM 1347 above.

Preservation and colour: The upper part of the stela is broken off. The surviving portion is well preserved apart from a few gouges and scratches on the surface. There are traces of yellow paint on the disk, solar bark, hieroglyphs, kilt of the figure and on the dividing lines between the columns of text.

Bibliography: *Sculpture Guide* (1909), 138 (no. 489); *HT* 7, pl. 38; Porter and Moss, *Top. Bibl.* I^{2}, ii, 730–1.

1. Undoubtedly Deir el-Medina on internal evidence.

Plates 40–41

1. Stela 286

Date: Ramesside
Provenance: Not recorded[1]
Date of acquisition: 1843 (Belmore collection)
Material: Limestone
Dimensions: 15.2 cm *h.*, 25 cm *w.*

The upper part of a round-topped stela with figures in sunk relief and incised texts is preserved. A workman on the right is worshipping Ptah who stands on the left behind an altar heaped with offerings.

Preservation and colour: The surviving portion of this stela is well preserved. There are traces of blue paint on the outside border and red paint in the hieroglyphs and dividing lines between the columns. Traces of blue paint are on the cap, beard and hands of Ptah, green paint on his face and sceptre, and red paint on his body. Traces of red paint are on the male figure and a pink shadow indicates his collar. Traces of green and blue paint appear on the floral bouquet on the altar and red paint on the other offerings.

Bibliography: *Sculpture Guide* (1909), 148 (no. 533); *HT* 7, pl. 41; Porter and Moss, *Top. Bibl.* I^{2}, ii, 736.

1. Undoubtedly Deir el-Medina on internal evidence.

2. Stela of *Ḥwy* 446

Date: Nineteenth Dynasty
Provenance: Not recorded[1]
Date of acquisition: Not recorded[2]
Material: Limestone
Dimensions: 24.5 cm *h.*, 60 cm *w.*

This partially preserved stela bears the remains of a scene carved in sunk relief on its upper edge, and below it five horizontal lines of incised hieroglyphs. The scene appears to be divided into two sections, one on the left and one on the right. On the left a male figure stands before four figures seated in chairs whose legs end in lion's paws and behind whom stands a female figure. On the right a female figure appears to stand before six figures seated on similar chairs. The text consists of a prayer to Osiris, Ptah-Sokar, Hathor, Harsiese, Amenhotep I and Ahmes-Nerfertari on behalf of the workman Huy, son of *Sbꜣ* and *Nfrt-ii.ti*. His wife *Tꜣḫꜣr* and his daughter *Dwꜣ-m-mr.st* are also named. The six figures on the right of the scene can probably be identified with the above-named deities.

The workman Huy was the owner of tomb no. 339 and is known from several other monuments (Porter and Moss, *Top. Bibl.* I², i, 406–7; B. Letellier, *Rev. d'Ég.* 27 (1975), 150–63; *KRI* III, 789–94). His daughter married the chiseller Ipuy, son of Piay, and thus, as a contemporary of Piay, Huy flourished during the reign of Sethos I and the early part of the reign of Ramesses II (Bierbrier, *Late New Kingdom*, 122, note 20, where for 'Nefertiry' read 'Nefertiti').

Preservation and colour: The surviving portion of this stela is in good condition apart from two gouges in the centre and on the right edge which is worn and partly broken away. The gouge in line 3 over the *sty* sign has enlarged since the photograph was taken with the loss of the plural strokes and part of the *di* sign. There are no traces of colour.

Bibliography: *Sculpture Guide* (1909), 104 (no. 357); *HT* 6, pl. 39; Porter and Moss, *Top. Bibl.* I², ii, 720; *KRI* III, 793.

1. Undoubtedly Deir el-Medina on internal evidence.
2. Possibly 1834 (Sams collection).

Plates 42–43

Head-rest of *Ḳn-ḥr-ḫpš.f* 63783

Date: Nineteenth Dynasty
Provenance: Not recorded[1]
Date of acquisition: 1933
Material: Limestone
Dimensions: 18.8 cm *h.*, 23 cm *w.*, 9.7 cm *deep*

This head-rest has been carved from a stone block in such a way as to leave a panel on each side of the shaft. The panels are decorated with figures in raised relief, while a column of text is incised down the shaft of the head-rest on each side. On one side (A) a figure of Bes is carved on the two panels. That on the right carries a spear in one hand and a snake in the other, while two serpents emerge from his mouth. The figure on the left is largely destroyed but enough survives to show that he carried a serpent in one hand. The text in the centre contains a prayer on behalf of the royal scribe Kenherkhepeshef. The other side of the head-rest (B) bears reliefs of fabulous creatures – a griffin on the left and a lioness(?) on the right. The text carries another prayer for Kenherkhepeshef. The outside edges of the head-rest were also incised with texts, but only one side (C) has survived, naming Kenherkhepeshef, son of *Pꜣ-[nḫt]*.

The owner of this head-rest can be identified with Kenherkhepeshef, the royal scribe of the Place of Truth, son of Panakht and adopted son of the scribe Ramose. He flourished from at least year 40 of Ramesses II until the reign of Sety II (Černý, *Community*, 329–37; Bierbrier, *Late New Kingdom*, 26–8). The head-rest, which was not intended to be functional, presumably formed part of his funerary equipment from his as yet undiscovered tomb.

Preservation and colour: The head-rest is not well preserved. It has been badly battered and the left side is largely destroyed. The surviving portion is much worn and covered in places with black paint, possibly discoloured. There are traces of blue paint inside some of the hieroglyphs.

Bibliography: *BMQ* 8 (1932–4), 105–7; M. L. Bierbrier, *The Tomb-builders of the Pharaohs* (London, 1982), fig. 49.

1. Ascribed to Deir Mawas presumably on the authority of the dealer Nahman from whom it was purchased. This alleged provenance is found in the BM register but not in the report of its purchase to the Trustees. From the name of the owner it is clear that this object must have come from Deir el-Medina or its vicinity.

Plates 44–45

1. Relief fragment 69089

Date: Nineteenth Dynasty
Provenance: Egypt[1]
Date of acquisition: 1979[2]
Material: Limestone
Dimensions: 11.8 cm *h.*, 26.5 cm *w.*

This fragment from a lintel or possibly a large stela is carved in sunk relief with incised texts. The upper parts of three male figures are depicted, the first carrying incense and the other two with floral offerings. Nine columns of text remain, the first and last being fragmentary. The text names 'his' brother, the workman *Ḳꜣḥꜣ*; 'his' brother, the stone-mason *ʾIiꜣ*; the lady *Twy*; and her daughter *Tnt-ʾIm[ntt]*.

The workman Kaha and his brother Iia are well known as sons of the workman Huy and his wife Tanehes from Deir el-Medina (Bierbrier, *Late New Kingdom*, 36–7). Tuy is known to have been Kaha's wife and Tentamentet was his daughter. Kaha was promoted to chief workman by year 38 of Ramesses II, so this inscription must have been carved before then. A list of Kaha's monuments can be conveniently consulted in *KRI* III, 598–609. Kaha had three other known brothers: Hay, owner of tomb 328, Huynufer and Paherpedjet, but it is likely that this fragment is part of a stela of Hay, one other piece of which is known (Bruyère, *Deir el-Médineh* (1929), 39, fig. 14, no. 12). The first male figure would then be Hay himself.

Preservation and colour: The piece is well preserved apart from gouges about the edges. There are no traces of colour.

Bibliography: *KRI* VII, 37; M. L. Bierbrier, *Studies in Egyptology Presented to Miriam Lichtheim* (Jerusalem, 1990), Vol. I, 63–9.

1. Undoubtedly Deir el-Medina on internal evidence.
2. Formerly in the Victoria and Albert Museum and before that in the Museum of Practical Geology (now the Geological Museum) to which it was presented in 1871 by Mrs Walker.

2. Lintel with *Ḏḥwty-ḥr-[mkt.]f* 547

Date: Nineteenth Dynasty
Provenance: Thebes[1]
Date of acquisition: 1843 (Belmore collection)
Material: Limestone
Dimensions: 23 cm *h.*, 37 cm *w.*

This fragment of a lintel is decorated in sunk relief with incised texts of which twelve columns survive. Osiris is enthroned on the left behind an altar heaped with offerings. The text also names the goddess Hathor, but no representation of her is preserved. On the right of the altar stands the necropolis-workman Djehuther[maktu]f with his arms raised in adoration. The text refers to him as [his] son. He is followed by a young girl, an adult female and another young girl who are named as his daughter *Nhyh3y*, [his wife?] *Wr[nr]* and [his daughter *Nfrt(?)]-ii.ti*.

Djehuthermaktuf, son of Nebdjefau, is a well-attested member of the community of Deir el-Medina in the early part of the reign of Ramesses II. A list of his monuments can be conveniently consulted in *KRI* III, 839–44 and G. Andreu, *BIFAO* 85 (1985), 1–21. His wife is named as the lady Werner, and she can be identified as the adult female on this lintel, the name of whom is more fully preserved in *Belmore Collection*, pl. 11. The young girls are thus the daughters of Djehuthermaktuf, although not attested elsewhere. Because of the reference to 'son' in the description of Djehuthermaktuf, this piece probably comes from the tomb of his father Nebdjefau.

Preservation and colour: Only a fragment of the original relief survives and it is much worn. Parts of the figures have been restored in modern times.

Bibliography: *Belmore Collection*, pl. 11; Maspero, *Rec. trav.* 11 (1880), 199; *Sculpture Guide* (1909), 142–3 (no. 505); *HT* 7, pl. 22; Porter and Moss, *Top. Bibl.* I², ii, 738; *KRI* III, 842; G. Andreu, *BIFAO* 85 (1985), 13–14.

1. Undoubtedly Deir el-Medina on internal evidence.

Plates 46–47

1. Stela of *Ḏḥwty.ḥr.mkt.f* 266

Date: Nineteenth Dynasty
Provenance: Thebes[1]
Date of acquisition: 1843 (Belmore collection)
Material: Limestone
Dimensions: 54.3 cm *h.*, 37 cm *w.*

This round-topped stela is divided into two sections decorated in sunk relief with incised texts. In the upper register the hawk-headed Re^{c}-Harakhty is seated in a solar bark together with a baboon on his left offering an *udjat*-eye to the god. The second register consists of ten columns of text which contain a prayer to Re^{c} on behalf of the workman Djehuthermaktuf who is depicted kneeling in adoration in the left-hand corner of the stela.

For the workman Djehuthermaktuf see pls. 44–45 above.

Preservation and colour: The upper and lower right-hand corners of the stela have been lost and restored in modern times. The surviving upper register is badly worn in places. There are extensive traces of orange paint on the figures in both registers and in the hieroglyphs.

Bibliography: *Belmore Collection*, pl. 14; Maspero, *Rec. trav.* 11 (1880), 198–9; *Sculpture Guide* (1909), 137 (no. 486); *HT* 7, pl. 37; Porter and Moss, *Top. Bibl.* I², ii, 718; *KRI* III, 841; G. Andreu, *BIFAO* 85 (1985), 14.

1. Undoubtedly Deir el-Medina on internal evidence.

2. Stela of *'Ipy* 332

Date: Nineteenth Dynasty
Provenance: Not recorded[1]
Date of acquisition: 1823 (Salt collection)
Material: Limestone
Dimensions: 36.3 cm *h.*, 24.3 cm *w.*

This round-topped stela is divided into two registers decorated in sunk relief and with incised texts. In the upper part the bark of Re^{c} is depicted, above which are seven columns of text. Below are eight columns of text consisting of a prayer to Re^{c} on behalf of the necropolis-workman Ipy who is shown kneeling on the right in adoration.

The name Ipy or Ipuy is not uncommon at Deir el-Medina. The owner of this stela is most likely to have been Ipuy, son of the sculptor Piay, whose name is occasionally spelled as Ipy, and who flourished in the first part of the reign of Ramesses II (Porter and Moss, *Top. Bibl.* I², ii, 721; Bierbrier, *JEA* 68 (1982), 89; *KRI* III, 660–5).

Preservation and colour: The stela is in a poor state of preservation. The surface is much worn and friable. There are several gouges along the edges, one of which has resulted in some loss to the beginning of the prayer in the lower register, while two others on the right side have been repaired in modern times. There are no traces of colour.

Bibliography: *Sculpture Guide* (1909), 139 (no. 493); *HT* 7, pl. 39; Porter and Moss, *Top. Bibl.* I², ii, 722.

1. Undoubtedly Deir el-Medina on internal evidence.

Plates 48–49

Votive figure of Renenutet 12247

Date: Ramesside
Provenance: Not recorded[1]
Date of acquisition: 1843 (Belmore collection)
Material: Wood
Dimensions: 6.5 cm *w.*, 12.2 cm *l.*, 10.8 cm *h.* (base), 4 cm *h.* (total)

This votive image consists of the lower part of a curled serpent on a pedestal which is now attached to a base bearing incised inscriptions on the top (A) and along the sides (B and C). The texts name the goddess Renenutet and the dedicatee of the figure, the necropolis-workman *B3k*.

The workman Bak cannot be identified precisely. It is possible that the name may be an abbreviated form of one of the numerous Bakenmuts, Bakenwerners and other like names in the community.

The base and serpent were acquired together as separate pieces said to be part of the same monument, but there is no absolute certainty that they should be joined together.

Preservation and colour: The upper part of the serpent was evidently carved as a separate piece to be joined to the body, but this is now lost. There is still some plaster adhering to the groove where the join was to be made. The base is worn along the edges and gouged in the rear. The hieroglyphs on the sides have been filled in originally in white which has now faded to yellow.

Bibliography: None.

1. Undoubtedly Deir el-Medina on internal evidence.

Plates 50–51

1. Stela of *'Imn-nḫt* 374

Date: Twentieth Dynasty
Provenance: Not recorded[1]
Date of acquisition: Not recorded
Material: Limestone
Dimensions: 20.6 cm *h.*, 14.3 cm *w.*

There are seven columns of incised texts on the upper part of this round-topped stela and a scene in sunk relief at the bottom. The scribe of the Place of Truth Amennakhte kneels on the lower right in adoration before an altar heaped with offerings. On the left the goddess Meresger is enthroned holding a lotus flower in one hand and an *ankh*-sign in the other.

The scribe Amennakhte, son of Ipuy, is well known from Deir el-Medina. He was appointed to office in year 16 of Ramesses III and is last attested under Ramesses VI (Bierbrier, *Late New Kingdom*, 39–40; *KRI* V, 645–53, VI, 202–4, 376–9).

Preservation and colour: The stela is slightly worn but otherwise well preserved. The surface is marked in two places by nodules of flint which have interrupted the text. The body of Amennakhte is red, his wig black and his kilt apparently unpainted. Meresger wears a red gown, headdress, bangles and sun-disk and holds a red-stemmed lotus. Her wig is black, but the colour of her body has faded or was never painted. The throne is red and blue with orange in between. Traces of blue and red paint remain on the offerings. The dividing lines between the hieroglyphs are red, while the borders of the stela are black. There are no traces of colour on the hieroglyphs.

Bibliography: *Sculpture Guide* (1909), 150 (no. 541); HT 7, pl. 29.

1. Undoubtedly Deir el-Medina on internal evidence.

2. Stela of *Smn-tꜣwy* 279

Date: Ramesside
Provenance: Thebes[1]
Date of acquisition: 1843 (Belmore collection)
Material: Limestone
Dimensions: 45.2 cm *h.*, 30 cm *w.*

There are two scenes in sunk relief with incised texts on this round-topped stela. In the upper register Smentawy, the guardian of the Place of Truth, kneels in adoration on the right, holding a brazier in one hand, before Amen-Re^c and Mut enthroned on the left. In the lower register the goddess Meresger is enthroned on the left behind an altar on which rests a water-pot cooled by a lotus flower. The fan-bearer *'It-n-it.f* and his wife, the lady *Nfr*, kneel in adoration on the right. A column of text between the two figures names her(?) sister *Tꜣ-'Iwnw*, whose relationship is obscure.

The guardian Smentawy is otherwise unattested (Černý, *Community*, 158). However, an inscribed fragment from Deir el-Medina names a Smentawy as the son of the lady Meresger described as the daughter of a Wadjrenpet (Bruyère, *Deir el Médineh (1948–1951)*, 38). Now a Meresger is attested as the wife of the guardian Amenemone and the mother of the guardian Kenherkhepeshef who flourished at the beginning of the reign of Ramesses II (Černý, *Community*, 155). There is also a Wadjrenpet in the family, but that is the name of Amenemone's mother and so Meresger's mother-in-law. For the two Meresgers to be identical, the inscription would have to be interpreted as either a reference to Wadjrenpet as mother(-in-law) of Meresger or possibly as a mistake for <her> daughter Wadjrenpet, the granddaughter being named after her grandmother. It would be highly unlikely for Meresger to have had a mother and a mother-in-law both named Wadjrenpet. Thus there is a possibility that the guardian flourished under Ramesses II. However, a Smentawy is also attested at the end of the Nineteenth Dynasty or early in the Twentieth Dynasty and he could be the guardian (Černý, *Community*, 158).

Preservation and colour: The stela is well preserved apart from some gouges and scratches on the surface. The lower corners are slightly damaged. There are traces of red paint along the outlines of the figures, thrones and altars, and in the dividing lines between the columns of hieroglyphs.

Bibliography: *Belmore Collection*, pl. 16; Maspero, *Rec. Trav.* 11 (1880), 192; Lieblein, *Dictionnaire*, No. 683; *Sculpture Guide* (1909), 131 (no. 464); Bruyère, *Mert Seger*, fig. 81; *HT* 7, pl. 27; Porter and Moss, *Top. Bibl.* I^2, ii, 734; *KRI* III, 694.

1. Undoubtedly Deir el-Medina on internal evidence.

Plates 52–53

1. Stela with *Nb-nfr* 811

Date: Twentieth Dynasty
Provenance: Not recorded[1]
Date of acquisition: 1854 (Valentia collection)
Material: Limestone
Dimensions: 35.5 cm *h.*, 24.8 cm *w.*

This round-topped stela is divided into two registers with incised texts and scenes in sunk relief. In the upper part a standing male figure on the right offers incense to the deified Amenhotep I and Ahmes-Nefertari who are enthroned on the left. The name of the worshipper is lost in a break. In the lower register a male and female kneel in adoration followed by another male and female. They are named as the necropolis-workman Nebnefer; his son *P(ꜣ)-n-<Tꜣ>-wr(t)*; his wife, the lady *Ḥwt-ii*; and her son (*sic* for daughter) *<T> ꜣ-wrt-m-mḥ* (?). The inscriptions do not match the carved figures, while the texts are clumsily inscribed and exhibit numerous errors.

The name Nebnefer is extremely common, but is found associated with Pentaweret in several ostraca of the reigns of Ramesses IV or V (M. Gutgesell, *Die Datierung der Ostraka und Papyri aus Deir el-Medineh und ihre ökonomische Interpretation* (Hildesheim, 1983), 240, 264, 352, 355, 390). These name Pentaweret, son of Nebnefer (once), and Nebenefer, son of Pentaweret, although it is not clear which is the father or son of the other. The name Hutiy is also attested in the Twentieth Dynasty (Gutgesell, *op. cit.*, 95 and D. Valbelle, *La Tombe de Hay à Deir el-Médineh* (Cairo, 1975), 29). Thus this stela should probably depict workmen of Deir el-Medina during the Twentieth Dynasty, although they cannot all be precisely identified.

Preservation and colour: The stela is badly cracked across the surface and has numerous gouges. The upper edge has been damaged with loss of text. There are traces of red paint on the human figures and the wigs of the women. There are slight traces of black paint in the hieroglyphs. A large black line on the bottom of the stela is probably due to nineteenth-century mounting.

Bibliography: Lieblein, *Dictionnaire*, No. 567; *Sculpture Guide* (1909), 103–4 (no. 356); *HT* 6, pl. 35; J. Černý, *BIFAO* 27 (1927), 165–6, 199; Porter and Moss, *Top. Bibl.* I², ii, 730.

1. Undoubtedly Deir el-Medina on internal evidence.
2. Presented by A. Lyttleton Annesley.

2. Stela of *P(ꜣ)-n-nfrw* 812

Date: Ramesside
Provenance: Not recorded[1]
Date of acquisition: 1854 (Valentia collection)[2]
Material: Limestone
Dimensions: 31.2 cm *h.*, 21.4 cm *w.*

There are two registers on this round-topped stela decorated with scenes in sunk relief and incised texts. In the upper register the ram-headed Amen-Reᶜ is enthroned on the right on one side of an altar heaped with offerings. The goddess Werethekau in the form of a serpent is entwined around a lotus flower on the left side of the altar. Behind her a small *was*-sceptre carries a large floral bouquet in its arms. In the lower register eight columns of text contain a prayer to Amen-Reᶜ and Werethekau on behalf of the guardian of the Place of Truth Pennefru.

Černý has conjectured that the name of this stela is a faulty rendering of Penmennefer, who is a well-attested guardian under Ramesses III (Černý, *Community*, 156). Certainly the stela exhibits other peculiarities such as the inverted *iod* in the first reference to Amun in the first column of the second register.

Preservation and colour: The stela is badly gouged in several places on the surface which has gone brown. There are traces of red paint in the lines between the columns of text and on the serpent, the flowers and the body and feathers of the headdress of Amen-Reᶜ, while black paint is visible on the horns of the god. There is a black nodule of flint embedded in the area where the throne of Amen-Reᶜ is delineated.

Bibliography: *Sculpture Guide* (1909), 143 (no. 506); *HT* 7, pl. 26; Bruyère, *Mert Seger*, fig. 93; Porter and Moss, *Top. Bibl.* I², ii, 732.

1. Undoubtedly Deir el-Medina on internal evidence.
2. Presented by A. Lyttleton Annesley.

Plates 54–55

1. Stela 270

Date: Ramesside
Provenance: Not recorded[1]
Date of acquisition: 1843 (Belmore collection)
Material: Limestone
Dimensions: 23.3 cm *h.*, 15.3 cm *w.*

There are two parts to this small, round-topped stela. In the upper section two busts are inset into the stela embedded in a layer of plaster. In the lower register a scene has been outlined in black ink with traces of the red ink draft in some areas. On the right a female apparently kneels in adoration of a large bust on a pedestal on the left. There were some short columns of text in black ink above the figure, but these are largely illegible.

Preservation and colour: The stela is in a poor state of preservation. The surface is very worn with the loss of much of the plaster surface in the upper part, and the top of the columns of text in the second register. The rest of the lower register has faded badly. There is a large gouge near the bottom of the stela, and the upper edge of the stela is badly chipped. The faces of the two inlaid busts are painted red. There are traces of blue paint on the cap and lower body of the bust on the right, and traces of red paint on the front of the bust on the left, while its cap may have been black. There is a black border along the edges of the stela and between the two registers.

Bibliography: *Sculpture Guide* (1909), 246 (no. 912).

1. Probably Deir el-Medina where other ancestral busts have been found (J. Keith-Bennett, *Bulletin of the Egyptological Seminar* 3 (1981), 43–72).

2. Stela fragment 277

Date: Ramesside
Provenance: Thebes[1]
Date of acquisition: 1843 (Belmore collection)
Material: Limestone
Dimensions: 21 cm *h.*, 32.5 cm *w.*

On the upper portion of a round-topped stela the figures of Amenhotep I and Ahmes-Nefertari are carved in sunk relief. They are enthroned before an altar on which rests a water-pot and other offerings. All texts are incised.

Preservation and colour: The lower portion of this stela is lost. The upper surviving part is damaged along the edges and scratched and gouged on the surface. There are no traces of colour.

Bibliography: *Belmore Collection*, pl. 11; *Sculpture Guide* (1909), 101 (no. 349); *HT* 6, pl. 34; J. Černý, *BIFAO* 27 (1927), 165, fig. 1; Porter and Moss, *Top. Bibl.* I², ii, 736.

1. Probably Deir el-Medina.

Plates 56–57

Lintel of Amenhotep I and Thutmose III 153

Date: Ramesside
Provenance: Thebes
Date of acquisition: 1843 (Belmore collection)
Material: Sandstone
Dimensions: 60 cm *h.*, 137 cm *l.*

There are two distinct scenes carved in sunk relief on either side of this stone slab. On the left King Thutmose III is offering Maat to Amen-Reᶜ, Mut, Khons and Hathor who are enthroned behind an altar on which rests a water-pot cooled by lotus flowers. On the right King Amenhotep I makes an offering of ointment jars to Amen-Reᶜ (here depicted as having a ram's head), Khnum, Selkis and Anukis who are all enthroned behind a similar altar. All texts are incised in columns above the heads of the figures.

This lintel possibly comes from a chapel dedicated to these deified kings at Deir el-Medina.

Preservation and colour: The stone is much worn on the surface and battered about the edges, with slight loss on the left side sustained in modern times. There are no traces of colour. The text on the left side has been restored from copies by Hawkins and Birch.

Bibliography: *Belmore Collection*, pls. 2–3; S. Sharpe, *Egyptian Antiquities in the British Museum* (London, 1862), 29, no. 153; *Sculpture Guide* (1909), 107 (no. 369); *HT* 6, pl. 42; J. Černý, *BIFAO* 27 (1927), 165, 170–1, 199; Porter and Moss, *Top. Bibl.* I², ii, 737; W. Murnane, *Ancient Egyptian Coregencies* (Chicago, 1977), 219; D. Valbelle, *Satis et Anoukis* (Mainz, 1981), 29, no. 252.

Plates 58–59

1. Stela of *Ptḥ-nḫt* 288

Date: Ramesside
Provenance: Abydos
Date of acquisition: 1835 (Salt collection)[1]
Material: Limestone
Dimensions: 50 cm *h.*, 31 cm *w.*

This round-topped stela is divided into three registers with figures in sunk relief and incised texts. In the upper part Osiris is seated on the left. Isis and Nephthys were intended to stand behind his throne, but only the figure of Nephthys has been carved with an extra arm representing Isis standing behind her. On the right stand in worship the guardian of writings Ptahnakhte, the chief guardian *Ḥwy*, and the lady *Nꜣiꜣ*. Above them eight columns of text name the figures.

In the second register one man and seven females are kneeling. The name of *'Iim* is squeezed above the male figure. Twelve columns of text name the ladies *Tꜣy*, *Mwt-m-wsḫt*, *Mryt-Ptḥ*, *Rnw(t)*, *Bꜣk(t)-Mwt*, *Tꜣ-mi(t)*, *Bꜣk(t)-Mwt* and *Mwt-m-wiꜣ*; and the chantress of Amun *Mryt-Ptḥ*. The names exceed the number of carved figures.

In the third register six male and two female figures are depicted in a similar attitude below eleven columns of text. They are named as the scribe *P(ꜣ)-n-grw*, the scribe *Rꜥ-ms*, the scribe of the chancellery *Ḥwy*, the guardian *Ptḥ-ms*, the guardian *P(ꜣ-n)-grw*, the scribe *Nfr-rnpt*, the chantress of Amun *Tꜣ-nḥs*, and the chantress of Amun *Tꜣ-kꜣri*.

These individuals cannot be further identified.

Preservation and colour: The stela has been slightly damaged by small gouges on the surface, and the edges are battered. Traces of red paint remain on the bodies of the figures and in some of the hieroglyphs. There are traces of orange in the pedestal of the throne of Osiris.

Bibliography: *Sculpture Guide* (1909), 242 (no. 888).

1. Lot 434, Sotheby sale 29 June 1835.

2. Stela of *Nḫt-mnw* 292

Date: Nineteenth–Twentieth Dynasty
Provenance: Not recorded
Date of acquisition: Not recorded
Material: Limestone
Dimensions: 50 cm *h.*, 39 cm *w.*

This round-topped stela is divided into three registers. All figures are in sunk-relief and all texts are incised. In the upper register Osiris is enthroned on the left and behind him stands Isis. In front of Osiris stands an altar on which rests a water-pot cooled by a lotus blossom. On the right are three figures standing in an attitude of adoration: Nakhtmin, who bears an obscure military title; his wife, the chantress of Amen-Reꜥ *Tꜣ-ꜥn(t)-ḥr-twy-st* (?), and *Pꜣ-mr-iḥw*, who bears the same title as Nakhtmin but whose relationship to him is not specified.

In the remaining registers the four sons (suffix *f* omitted) and the six daughters of Nakhtmin are shown standing with arms raised in worship. In the middle register are the army scribe *Wsr-mꜣꜥt-rꜥ-nḫt*, the *wꜥb*-priest of the temple of Reꜥ-Harakhty *'Iꜣ*, the *wꜥb*-priest *Ns-'Imn*, *Nḫt-Mnw*, and *ꜣst-wrt*. In the lower register appear *Ḳꜣy-tꜣ-nḫb(t)*, *Ns-Rꜥ*, *Pꜣ-tꜣ-ḥrr*, *ꜥnkt-m-ḥb*, and *Wrt-nfrt*.

Preservation and colour: The stela is well preserved apart from the loss of the lower right corner. There are no traces of colour.

Bibliography: *Sculpture Guide* (1909), 194 (no. 703).

Plates 60–61

1. Stela of *P(ꜣ)-n-'Imn* 309

Date: Ramesside
Provenance: Abydos
Date of acquisition: 1835 (Salt collection)[1]
Material: Limestone
Dimensions: 47 cm *h.*, 32.8 cm *w.*

There are three registers on this round-topped stela with incised texts and figures in sunk relief. In the upper register Osiris is enthroned in the centre behind an altar heaped with offerings. Isis and Harsiese stand behind him. On the right the scribe of divine books, god's chancellor and *it-nṯr* priest of Reꜥ-Atum in the house of life Penamun, born of *Mwt-m-wsḫt*, stands in adoration.

There is a pile of offerings in the centre of the second register. On the left squats the royal scribe and lector-priest Penamun followed by his father *Nꜣ-ḥr-ḥr* and the lady *Twy*. On the right squats the scribe *'Ibwdb*, the lady of the house *Mwt-m-wsḫt* and her mother *Ḥnwt-nfrt*. There is a similar scene in the third register consisting of squatting female figures on either side of a pile of offerings. On the right are his sister *Twy*, his sister *Nfrt-iry*, and his sister *Bꜣkt-Ptḥ*, while on the left sit his sister the chantress of the lady of the Sycomore *Twy*, his sister *Nhy* and his sister *Tꜣ-wrt-ḥtp.ti*.

The genealogy of this family is not entirely clear. Presumably the lady Mutemweskhet in the second register should be identified as the mother of the scribe Penamun. It would seem that the scribe Ibudeb who precedes her ought to be her consort, but the text states that Naherher, who immediately follows Penamun, is his father and hence husband of Mutemweskhet. Ibudeb could then be his brother or possibly maternal grandfather as Henutnefret is certainly his maternal grandmother. The lady Tuy remains unplaced, but is possibly the wife of Penamun. Certainly the chantress Tuy in the third register ought to be his wife, while the other ladies could well be his actual sisters.

Preservation and colour: The stela is well preserved apart from a few small gouges on the surface and some damage along the edges. There are no traces of colour.

Bibliography: *Sculpture Guide* (1909), 210 (no. 762).

1. Lot 432, Sotheby sale 29 June 1835.

2. Stela of *Bȝk-n-'Imn* 349

Date: Nineteenth–Twentieth Dynasty
Provenance: Not recorded
Date of acquisition: Not recorded
Material: Sandstone
Dimensions: 75 cm *h.*, 38 cm *w.*

This stela consists of an inner round-topped stela of three registers surmounted by a pyramidal projection on which a jackal is depicted. All texts are incised and figures are carved in sunk relief. In the upper register of the stela Osiris is seated on a throne on the left and behind him stands Isis with one arm raised. In front of Osiris stands an altar heaped with food offerings. On the right stands the table-scribe of the wine cellar Bakenamun, with his arms raised in worship, and behind him his wife, the lady of the house and chantress of Amun *Wrt-wȝḥ-sw*, is shown holding a sistrum in one hand.

The lower registers depict a series of male and female figures standing in an attitude of worship. The women usually have a sistrum on a lotus flower in one hand, but in one case both are carried and in one instance the lady holds a vessel. In the second register the individuals are named as the *wʿb*-priest of Amun of the wine cellar *'Imn-m-ipt*, father of Bakenamun; his (Bakenamun's) mother, the chantress *'Inihȝy*; his son, the *wʿb*-priest *Pȝ-rʿ-m-ḥb*; his son, the workman *Pȝ-sr*; and his son, the workman *'Imn-ḫʿw*. In the third register appear his son, the workman *Ḥwy*; his daughter, the chantress *Nfrt-iry*; his daughter, the chantress *ȝst*; his daughter, the chantress *Tȝ-kȝrt*; his daughter *Mwt-m-'Iwnw*; and his daughter, the chantress *Ḫʿt-bȝḫt*.

Preservation and colour: The stela is in an excellent state of preservation. There are no traces of colour.

Bibliography: Lieblein, *Dictionnaire*, no. 679; *Sculpture Guide* (1909), 206 (no. 751).

Plates 62–63

Stela of *Ḫȝr* 549

Date: Nineteenth–Twentieth Dynasty
Provenance: Not recorded
Date of acquisition: 1839 (Anastasi collection)[1]
Material: Limestone
Dimensions: 100 cm *h.*, 40 cm *w.*

This round-topped stela is divided into three registers with incised texts and figures in sunk relief. In the upper register Osiris and Isis stand on the left behind an altar covered with offerings. On the right stand Khar, the maker of runners of the kitchen of pharaoh, and *Ḥnr*, the chantress of Amun, with their arms raised in worship.

In the middle register Anubis, standing on the left, clasps the upright mummy of Khar. Two women, *Wrt-nfrt* and Huner are mourning over the mummy. In the centre stands a pile of offerings and on the right four women and two men stand in an attitude of mourning: *ʿn-Mwt*, *Tȝ-ṯhrt*, *Ḥnwt-mtr*, *Tȝ-wrt-ḥtp.ti*, *Bȝk-n-Mwt*, and *Pȝ-nfr*. In the bottom register Khar and Huner are seated on the left behind an altar. On the right stand his daughter *Tȝ-rnw* and his sons *Ms*, *Ptḥ-pȝ-...*, *Ptḥ*(?)... and *Bȝk-n-wrn(r)*.

This family appears to be otherwise unknown. There is some uncertainty as to the meaning of Khar's title, *ir wȝt šwy n tȝ wʿbt n pr ʿȝ*. The phrase *wȝt šwy* is usually translated as 'runner' or 'long mat of dried grass' (A. H. Gardiner, *Ancient Egyptian Onomastica* (Oxford, 1947), I, no. 137 and J. Janssen, *Commodity Prices from the Ramessid Period* (Leiden, 1975), 154, note 96). On this stela the *wȝt šwy* is definitely associated with the *wʿbt*, which is usually translated as 'kitchen'.

Preservation and colour: The stela is badly flaked and worn. Traces of red paint remain on the robe of Isis, the body of Anubis, the bodies of Khar and Huner in the bottom register, and in the dividing lines between the columns of text. There are also traces of a blue border around the stela.

Bibliography: Lieblein, *Dictionnaire*, no. 679; *Sculpture Guide* (1909), 186 (no. 670).

1. Erroneously ascribed to the Salt collection by Budge in *Sculpture Guide* (1909), 186 (no. 670).

Plates 64–65

Stela of *Mr-ptḥ-(m)-pr-'Imn* 350

Date: Ramesside
Provenance: Said to be Thebes[1]
Date of acquisition: 1837 (Athanasi collection)[2]
Material: Sandstone
Dimensions: 53.5 cm *h.*, 38 cm *w.*

This crudely carved, round-topped stela bears two registers on each side. The upper register of the first side (A) shows Amen-Reʿ enthroned in the centre with Mut and Khons standing behind. An altar on which rests a water-pot cooled by a lotus flower is situated before the god. On the right Merptah(em)peramun stands in adoration with a brazier in one hand. An upstanding lotus is depicted behind him. In the lower register a prayer to Amen-Reʿ and Mut is incised on behalf of Merptah(em)-peramun, son of *Ptrm* (?). He is depicted standing in adoration along with the lady *Mtr*, who holds a lotus and sistrum, and his son *Rʿ-mss-m-pr-'Itm*, who holds a lotus. The lady is evidently the wife of Merptah(em)peramun.

On the second side of the stela the upper register depicts Ramessem(per)atum, who may possibly be also known as *Ptḥ-(m)-wiȝ*, although the context is unclear. He is shown in adoration on the right of the scene before an altar heaped with offerings. Beyond the altar Osiris sits on his throne behind which stands Isis and the standard of the West. In the lower register Amen-Reʿ stands on the left behind an altar on which rests a water-pot cooled by a lotus flower. He is worshipped by *Mr-mšʿ.f*, otherwise known as *Pȝ-pr-ʿȝ-(r-)nḥḥ*, a lady holding a lotus and a sistrum beside whom is the text 'her daughter *Rn*, and Ramessemperatum.

No further details are available on this family group. The main title used by the family is obscure.

Preservation and colour: The stela shows signs of wear on the surface. The bottom edge is damaged. There are traces of red paint on the figure of Mut, the throne of Amun, the altar and the figure of the deceased in the upper register of side A.

Bibliography: *Sculpture Guide* (1909), 206 (no. 749).

1. According to the sale catalogue.
2. Lot 704, Sotheby sale 13 March 1837.

Plates 66–67

1. Stela of *'Imn-ms* 351

Date: Ramesside
Provenance: Not recorded
Date of acquisition: Not recorded
Material: Sandstone
Dimensions: 69.3 cm *h.*, 38.5 cm *w.*

This round-topped stela consists of three registers carved in sunk relief with incised texts. In the upper section the scribe Amenmose, son of the dignitary *R^c-(m-)wiꜣ*, stands on the right in worship of Osiris who is enthroned in the centre. Behind the god stands Isis, and, behind her, Horus is depicted in the form of a hawk perched on a *djed*-pillar. An altar on which rests a water-pot cooled by a lotus flower is placed between the figure of Amenmose and the seated god.

In the second register four male figures face left with arms raised in adoration, the last of which carries a lotus flower in one hand. The first is identified as the scribe *'Imn-m-wiꜣ*, son of the dignitary *'Iwnw*. The phrase 'of the pure storehouse' which appears in the next column refers without doubt to the scribal post of Amenemwia and not to that of his father. The others are named as the *w^{c}b*-priest *'Iwnꜣiꜣ*, the scribe *Mḥy* and the *w^{c}b*-priest *'Iwnꜣiꜣ*.

The third register consists of five females facing left. The first has both arms raised in adoration, while the others raise one arm and carry a vase or flower in the other. The first is identified with the phrase 'born of the chantress of Amun, *Twy*'. As this continues the filiation of Amenemwia from the previous register, she is presumably his mother. The others are the chantress of Amun *Mwt-m-wiꜣ*; the chantress of Amun *Bꜣk(t)-'Imn*; the chantress of Amun *Tyiꜣy* (?); and the chantress of Amun . . . *Mwt*. The names of the last two are unclear.

The relationship of all these figures is obscure. Evidently Amenemwia is the son of Iunu and Tuy, but it is not clear how he is related to Amenmose unless the latter's father, Re^c(em)wia, is to be identified with him. One of the two *w^{c}b*-priests, Iunaia, is possibly the father of Amenemwia. Otherwise the family remains unknown.

Preservation and colour: The stela is slightly damaged at the top and has been battered on the bottom, which has been restored in modern times. The stela is worn in places, so the hieroglyphs are not always clearly defined. There are no traces of colour.

Bibliography: *Guide* (1922), 195 (no. 711).

2. Naos of *Ḫ^c-m-ipt* 472

Date: Nineteenth Dynasty
Provenance: Not recorded
Date of acquisition: 1845 (Athanasi collection)[1]
Material: Limestone
Dimensions: 49 cm *h.* (unrestored), 25.5 cm *w.*, 22.5 cm *deep*

The front of this naos consists of a doorway within which appears a standing figure carved in raised relief. He holds in his right hand a standard of Osiris and in his left hand a standard surmounted by the head of Re^c or Re^c-Harakhty. Along the lintel and jambs are incised dedications to Osiris on behalf of the table-scribe of the lord of the two lands, Khaemopet, otherwise unknown. The other three sides of the naos are uninscribed.

Preservation and colour: The bottom of the naos has been damaged and restored in modern times. The edges are chipped with minor loss to some signs. There are no traces of colour.

Bibliography: *Sculpture Guide* (1909), 201 (no. 729); O. Koefoed-Petersen in *Miscellanea Gregoriana* (Vatican, 1941), 123, fig. 5, and 125–6; H. Satzinger in W. F. Reineke, *Acts of the First International Congress of Egyptology* (Berlin, 1979), 565 and note 2; C. Chadefaud, *Les Statues Porte-Enseignes de l'Égypte ancienne* (Paris, 1982), 120–1.

1. Lot 153,2 in the sale catalogue (Sotheby, 17 July 1845). The attribution to the Barker collection in *Sculpture Guide* (1909), 201 (no. 729), is erroneous.

Plates 68–69

1. Fragment of a stela or tomb relief 455

Date: Nineteenth–Twentieth Dynasty
Provenance: Thebes
Date of acquisition: 1823 (Salt collection)
Material: Limestone
Dimensions: 44.5 cm *h.*, 62.3 cm *w.*

This fragment bears part of a scene carved in shallow sunk relief over a thin layer of plaster. All texts are incised. The god Anubis sits on his customary shrine-shaped pedestal facing left. In front of him is an altar on which rests a water-pot cooled by lotus blossoms. On the left edge of the slab are the remains of a parallel Anubis facing right. Five columns of text appear at the top of the fragment. The upper right corner of the slab is abraded. This stela was either free-standing or, more likely, part of a tomb relief.

Preservation and colour: Apart from some loss of signs on the upper right edge, this fragment is in a good state of preservation with the original colour largely intact. The body of the jackal is blue-black, his collar and flail yellow with red details and his sash red. The shrine-shaped pedestal is outlined in red with red and blue-green stripes on the architrave and a blue-green door edged in red. The altar and water-pot are yellow and the flowers blue with red stems. The hieroglyphs are painted red or blue with red dividing lines between the columns.

Bibliography: *Sculpture Guide* (1909), 173 (no. 626).

2. Stela 646

Date: Ramesside
Provenance: Not recorded
Date of acquisition: Not recorded
Material: Limestone
Dimensions: 42 cm *h.*, 58 cm *w.*

Only the top of a round-topped stela has been preserved. The figures are in sunk relief and the texts are incised. There is an altar in the centre on which rests a water-pot cooled by lotus blossoms. On the right Amenresonther and Mut are enthroned, while on the left sit Horus lord of Hebenu, and Isis. Seven columns of text above the gods give their names and epithets.

The stela possibly comes from Hebenu, capital of the Gazelle nome, a site not definitely located but near Minya (*LÄ* II, 1075–6; D. Kessler, *Historische Topographie der Region zwischen Mallawi und Samalut* (Wiesbaden, 1981), 209–24).

Preservation and colour: The surviving part of this stela has been heavily battered about the edges. There is a great amount of wear on the surface, especially in the upper left-hand corner.

Bibliography: *Sculpture Guide* (1909), 173–4 (no. 629).

Plates 70–71

1. Stela of *Ḥr-mnw* 321

Date: Ramesside
Provenance: Not recorded
Date of acquisition: 1834 (Sams collection)
Material: Limestone
Dimensions: 39.5 cm *h.*, 34.5 cm *w.*

There are three sections to this round-topped stela. In the upper register the ship's captain, *Pꜣ-tꜣ* (?), kneels on the right in adoration of Osiris, Horus and Isis; before him is an altar on which rests a water-pot cooled by a lotus blossom. In the second register the follower Harmin, the lady of the house *ᶜꜣt-niwt*, the stable-master *Bꜣk-ᶜꜣ*, the porter[1] *'Ipy* and the lady of the house *Mry* squat in a row before a pile of offerings on the right. The third section of the register consists of a prayer in two lines to Osiris and Anubis on behalf of Harmin.

Preservation and colour: The edges of the stela are slightly damaged, and there are gouges on the surface. A nodule of rock remains in the left-hand lower corner. Traces of yellow can be seen on some of the figures.

Bibliography: *Sculpture Guide* (1909), 218 (no. 788).

1. For this title see J.-M. Kruchten, *Chron. d'Ég.* 60 (1985), 109–16.

2. Stela of *Twnn-nḫb-Ḫnsw* 700

Date: Ramesside
Provenance: Not recorded
Date of acquisition: 1905[1]
Material: Limestone
Dimensions: 31.5 cm *h.*, 22 cm *w.*

On the top of this round-topped stela is depicted a winged sun-disk carved in raised relief. Below, in sunk relief, the metal-engraver Tunennekhebkhons holds an offering before an altar piled with other offerings to the god Osiris who stands on the left. Behind the owner of the stela stands his wife the chantress of Amun *Ḥnwt-tꜣ-nb*, with her arms raised in worship. Seven columns of texts are incised above them, and three lines of text below the scene contain a prayer to Reᶜ-Harakhty, Osiris and Anubis on behalf of Tunennekhebkhons and his wife.

Preservation and colour: The stela is well preserved apart from a few gouges along the edges and on the surface. The lower right side has become darker than the rest of the stela. There are traces of red paint on the lower left edge, although this may not be original.

Bibliography: *Sculpture Guide* (1909), 205 (no. 745); R. Moss, *JEA* 27 (1941), 9, pl. II.

1. In the possession of the dealer Cureton *c.* 1830–40, but purchased from the Revd T. Philpot in 1905.

Plates 72–73

Stela of *Rᶜ-ms-sw-m-pr-Rᶜ* 796

Date: Nineteenth Dynasty
Provenance: Not recorded
Date of acquisition: 1858[1]
Material: Limestone
Dimensions: 63.5 cm *h.*, 38 cm *w.*

This round-topped stela is divided into four registers with figures in sunk relief and incised texts. In the centre of the upper register Osiris is seated upon a throne and behind him stand Isis, Horus, son of Isis,[2] and Thoth. In front of Osiris is a lotus blossom on which stand the four sons of Horus. On the right the chief guardian of the Ramesseum Ramesesemperreᶜ stands with his arms raised in adoration.

In the second register the goddess Nut stands in a tree on the right and pours a libation into the hands of the kneeling Ramesesemperreᶜ. Behind him sit five figures holding lotus blossoms: *Pꜣ-nḫt-m-ṯ* (?), *Ḥr-m-ḥꜣt*, *Swty-ms*, *Nfr-rnpt* and *Nḫt-m-Wꜣst*. In the third register six men and one woman are shown squatting on the ground and holding lotus blossoms: *Swr*, *Ḫnsw*, *Ḫnsw*, *P(ꜣ)-n-rnw*, *ꜣny*, *Ptḥ-m-ḥb* and *Ḥwt-Ḥr*. In the fourth register it is impossible to read anything apart from a few signs because it is too damaged, although Birch read the name of *Nfr-rnpt* in the nineteenth century. This register presumably consisted of more squatting or seated figures.

The guardian Ramesesemperreᶜ is otherwise unknown, but Schulman has suggested that he might be identified with a royal butler of this name who flourished under Merenptah and Ramesses III (Schulman, *JARCE* 13 (1976), 117–30). There is no firm evidence for this suggestion, and it is not certain that the royal butler under Merenptah is the same man under Ramesses III.

Preservation and colour: This stela is in an extremely poor state of preservation and has suffered much surface damage. More deterioration has occurred since the photograph used here was taken, and large parts of the stela are illegible. There are no traces of colour.

Bibliography: *Sculpture Guide* (1909), 195 (no. 110); J. Berlandini-Grenier, *BIFAO* 74 (1974), 15–19.

1. Lot 111 of an unrecorded sale at Stevens. A second stela with the same description recorded as lot 144 is probably confused with lot 111.
2. Read by Birch.

Plates 74–77

Naos of *'Imn-m-ḥb* 474

Date: Nineteenth–Twentieth Dynasty
Provenance: Not recorded
Date of acquisition: 1833 (Barker collection)[1]
Material: Limestone
Dimensions: 67 cm *h.*, 39 cm *w.*, 39 cm *deep*

This naos of the scribe of recruits and army scribe Amenemheb is decorated on three sides with figures in sunk relief and incised texts. On the front of the naos within the doorway stands a statue of Amenemheb in high relief holding a standard. The two jambs bear reliefs of Amenemheb and texts giving his name and titles (A). On the remains of the lintel are depicted the bark of Reᶜ being worshipped by a baboon and several conventional designs including an *udjat*-eye and the standard of Osiris, but half of the lintel is lost.

On the left side of the naos (B) Amenemheb and his wife the chantress of Amun *Tꜣ-nfrt*, stand with their arms raised in adoration. Behind them stand a male figure, whose filiation is lost but who is probably a son, *Nb-'Imn*, and beneath him the chantress of Monthu *Bꜣk(t)-wrn(r)*, probably a daughter. On the right side of the naos (C) Amenemheb and Tanefret appear in a similar posture. Behind them stand a *wꜥb*-priest of Monthu whose name is lost and beneath him a daughter named *Wrnr* holding a lotus flower. The stone is damaged before her name, so it is possible that she might be identified with the daughter on the right side if some signs have been lost.

An inscription containing two invocations (D and E) to Osiris and Horus on behalf of the army scribe Amenemheb and the scribe of recruits *Nhrti*, presumably an alternate name of Amenemheb, runs around three sides of the base of the naos. There are three fragmentary columns of text on the top of the shrine (F), one in the centre and one on each edge. The centre text contains the name of Amenemheb, and that on its left may have named his mother but is now damaged. The text on the other side is almost completely lost, but may have named his father.

Preservation and colour: The naos is badly damaged with losses to the front, sides and top. The surviving portion is severely cracked in places and the base inscription is nearly illegible in parts. There are no traces of colour.

Bibliography: *Sculpture Guide* (1909), 207 (no. 754); Vandier, *Manuel* III, 474, note 8; C. Chadefaud, *Les Statues Portes-Enseignes de l'Égypte ancienne* (Paris, 1982), 121–2, with wrong title.

1. Lot 241 in the sale catalogue (Sotheby, 16 March 1833).

Plates 78–79

Statue of *Pꜣ-mr-iḥw* 853

Date: Ramesside
Provenance: Not recorded
Date of acquisition: 1845 (Athanasi collection)[1]
Material: Limestone
Dimensions: 70 cm *h.* (unrestored), 34.7 cm *w.*, 44.7 cm *deep*

A large, naophorous block statue of the general Pamerihu who is depicted holding a lettuce in each hand and squatting on a cushion. Before him is a naos with the figure of Osiris inside. The naos has a winged disk carved in raised relief on its lintel and a *djed*-pillar on each jamb. On the lower edge a brief inscription is incised naming Osiris (A). Further texts are incised along the front and two sides (B, C), the top of the head of the statue (D) and the top of the naos (E) naming the royal scribe and general Pamerihu. The back pillar is not inscribed. The sides of the statue bear inscriptions in hieratic written in black ink, but these have so faded that they are no longer legible.

Preservation and colour: The statue has suffered extensive damage to its bottom which has been restored in modern times. The surviving portion is much worn and the surface cracked and gouged in several places. There are traces of red paint on the front and inner sides of the naos and black on the rear. The ink texts on the body of the statue have faded.

Bibliography: *Sculpture Guide* (1909), 179 (no. 644); Vandier, *Manuel* III, 461.

1. Lot 157, Sotheby sale 17 July 1845.

Plates 80–81

1. Stela of *Ḥri* 891

Date: Ramesside
Provenance: Not recorded
Date of acquisition: 1907
Material: Limestone
Dimensions: 29.5 cm *h.*, 20.8 cm *w.*

This small, round-topped stela consists of one scene in sunk relief above two lines of incised text. On the right the assault-officer of the garrison troops of pharaoh is standing in worship of the standard of Wepwawet in the centre before which is a large floral bouquet and behind which are depicted four wolves, one above the other.

The name of the owner of this stela has been earlier read as My, but Hori seems preferable. The carving of the inscription is somewhat clumsy and appears not to have been completed in the upper part because of lack of space. For the military title see A. Schulman, *Military Rank, Title and Organization in the Egyptian New Kingdom* (Berlin, 1964), 17–18, 57–8.

Preservation and colour: The stela is fairly well preserved apart from slight damage to the lower right corner which has been restored and some wear on the surface. The surface is covered with a large number of black smudges. There are traces of red paint on the arms and legs of the human figure, on the bouquet, the edge of the standard and in the dividing lines of the text in the upper scene. There are traces of black in some of the hieroglyphs in the lower text.

Bibliography: *Sculpture Guide* (1909), 246 (no. 915); P. Munro, *ZÄS* 88 (1963), 51–2, pl. v; J. Yoyotte and J. López, *Bi. Or.* 26 (1969), 17.

2. Stela of *Ḫnsw* 1430

Date: Ramesside
Provenance: Not recorded
Date of acquisition: 1908
Material: Limestone
Dimensions: 53.5 cm *h.*, 35.5 cm *w.*

This round-topped stela is divided into two sections with figures in sunk relief and incised texts. In the upper portion there are five registers, each consisting of a bowl of incense in the centre flanked by a wolf on either side. Above the bowl of incense is carved the name of Wepwawet. In the lower part of the stela there is an altar with offerings on the right before which kneel in adoration the chief stable-master Khons, his wife the lady of the house *Tꜣ-wr(t)*, and his son the scribe of the treasury of the lord of the two lands *Ḥri*.

Preservation and colour: The surface of the stela is worn in several places with some loss to the figures and texts.

Bibliography: *Sculpture Guide* (1909), 218 (no. 791); H. Bonnet, *Reallexikon der ägyptischen Religionsgeschichte* (Berlin, 1952), 321; P. Munro, *ZÄS* 88 (1963), 52, pl. v.

Plates 82–83

1. Stela of *Pꜣ-(n)-Tꜣ-wr(t)* 1632

Date: Nineteenth–Twentieth Dynasty
Provenance: Not recorded
Date of acquisition: 1926
Material: Limestone
Dimensions: 47.5 cm *h.*, 34 cm *w.*

This round-topped stela contains three main registers and a border at the bottom with figures in sunk relief and texts crudely incised. In the upper register on the right the standard of the god Wepwawet is carried on the shoulders of eleven (?) priests. In front of the standard are the *wʿb*-priest *ʾImn-ms*, and Pe(n)tawer(et) with their arms raised in adoration. Behind them are carved the figures of four wolves. In the second register Pe(n)tawer(et) is kneeling on the right pouring a libation before an altar covered with offerings. On the left a jackal-headed god is squatting and another jackal is seated on a pedestal. The text contains a prayer to Anubis.

In the main part of the lower register a ram-headed god stands on the right before an altar heaped with food offerings. On the left stands Wepwawet in human form with a wolf's head. He is spearing a crocodile which is carved below the level of the register and is chasing a human figure whose head projects above the border into the register. Behind Wepwawet are carved the figures of three wolves.

Preservation and colour: The stela is in a good state of preservation apart from some surface wear. There are no traces of colour.

Bibliography: H. Brunner, *MDAIK* 16 (1958), 5–19.

2. Stela of *Pyiꜣy* 1725

Date: Ramesside
Provenance: Not recorded
Date of acquisition: 1930
Material: Limestone
Dimensions: 29 cm *h.*, 23.5 cm *w.*

This small, round-topped stela bears incised texts and figures in sunk relief. Pyiay stands in the centre right of the stela holding a brazier in one hand and pouring a libation from the other over an altar piled with offerings. His wife *Ḥwt.ḥr* stands behind him holding more offerings. They are identified by three columns of text above the figures. On the other side of the altar is the standard of Wepwawet behind which are five wolves, one above the other.

The individuals cannot otherwise be identified.

Preservation and colour: The stela is well preserved apart from some gouges and scratches on the surface and some unevenness about the edges. There are traces of a black substance adhering to the surface in places.

Bibliography: *BMQ* 5 (1930–1), 18, pl. IXc; P. Munro, *ZÄS* 88 (1962), 52, pl. v.

Plates 84–85

1. Stela of *Stẖ-nẖt* 1831

Date: Nineteenth–Twentieth Dynasty
Provenance: Serabit el-Khadim
Date of acquisition: 1967
Material: Sandstone
Dimensions: 55 cm *h.*, 34 cm *w.*

The face of this round-topped stela is divided into two registers with figures in sunk relief and incised texts. In the upper register the goddess Hathor stands on the right and is being worshipped by a standing male figure above and beside whom are four columns of text. His name is now illegible but from an earlier copy (see bibliography) he can be identified as the royal scribe Sethnakhte, son of *ʿb-pdt*. In the lower register two female figures kneel in adoration. They are named as the chantress of Thoth *Tꜣy-bs*, and <her> daughter, the chantress of <Thoth> *Tꜣ-ʿḳy*, presumably Sethnakhte's wife and daughter.

Sethnakhte is known from one other monument at Serabit el-Khadim dated to year 3 (Gardiner and Peet, *The Inscriptions of Sinai*, 2nd ed., no. 301).

Preservation and colour: The state of preservation of this stela is not good. The surface is much worn in places and pitted. In two areas, one above the head of Sethnakhte and the other at the side of his figure, the surface has been treated with a restorative in modern times and subsequently scratched with the result that these areas are largely illegible.

Bibliography: Gardiner and Peet, *The Inscriptions of Sinai* I, 1st ed. (London, 1917), pl. LXXVI, no. 295; 2nd ed. (London, 1952), pl. LXXVI, no. 295; II (London, 1955), p. 193, no. 295; Porter and Moss, *Top. Bibl.* VII, 365.

2. Stela of *Nb-nfr* 1184

Date: Ramesside
Provenance: Not recorded
Date of acquisition: 1894
Material: Limestone
Dimensions: 67 cm *h.*, 38.5 cm *w.*

This round-topped stela is surmounted by a pyramidal superstructure on which are carved some convential designs flanked by *udjat*-eyes. The stela itself is divided into three registers carved in sunk relief and incised texts. In the upper register the chief follower of His Majesty Nebnefer kneels in adoration on the right before an altar on which rests a water-pot. Behind the altar is the standard of Wepwawet before an enthroned Osiris behind whom stand Horus and Isis. In the second register Nebnefer on the right offers incense and pours a libation over a pile of offerings. Facing him squatting on the ground are his father the herdsman *Wsr-ḥꜣt*; his son *Ḥʿp-ʿꜣ*; the chantress of Wepwawet *Tꜣ-wrt*; the lady of the house and chantress of Wepwawet *Sẖmt*; and the chantress of Wepwawet *Ḥpt-di-sw*(?). Nebnufer is similarly depicted in the third register with the facing figures of the follower of His Majesty *Wp-wꜣwt-ms*; the chantress of Wepwawet *Ḥwt.ḥr*; the follower of His Majesty *P(ꜣ)-n-Tꜣ-wrt*; a lady *Sꜣiꜣ*; and the chantress of Wepwawet *Nb(t)-tꜣwy*.

Preservation and colour: The stone used for the stela is uneven on the surface with a nodule sticking out on the upper right side. The top and edges of the stela have been damaged and there are several gouges on the surface. Traces of red paint remain on the bodies of the human figures and the legs of Horus.

Bibliography: *Sculpture Guide* (1909), 172 (no. 623).

Plates 86–87

Statue of *ȝšȝmriȝ* 1382

Date: Ramesside
Provenance: Not recorded[1]
Date of acquisition: 1835 (Salt collection)[2]
Material: Limestone
Dimensions: 48.5 cm *h.* (unrestored); 38.5 cm *h.* (stela, unrestored); 20 cm *w.*, 26.5 cm *deep*

A kneeling stelophorous statue of the chief altar attendant of Amun Ashamria, in a long linen skirt and wig and sporting a short beard. The stela consists of one scene at the top and six lines of incised text. Re^{c}-Harakhty is depicted in his bark, Horus at the rudder and Maat at the prow of the boat. A baboon is shown in an attitude of worship above the bark on either side. On the extreme right is a standard, and it and the bark rest on the sky-sign. The text consists of a prayer to Re^{c}-Harakhty on behalf of Ashamria. A column of text is incised down the back-pillar and rear base of the statue containing the usual *ḥtp-di-nsw* formula to Amen-Re^{c} for the deceased.

The owner of the statue cannot be further identified.

Preservation and colour: The statue and stela are fairly well preserved apart from some damage to the edges of the stela and the right arm and base of the statue. The broken base has been restored in modern times, as has the top right corner of the stela where some signs have been lost. These can be restored from early publications when this corner was still intact. The surface of the statue is slightly worn. There are traces of blue paint in the hieroglyphs and figures and red paint in the dividing lines between the text.

Bibliography: S. Sharpe, *Eg. Inscr.* 1st ser., pl. 46; *Sculpture Guide* (1909), 186 (no. 669); Vandier, *Manuel* III, 472; Porter and Moss, *Top. Bibl.* I^{2}, ii, 790.

1. *Sculpture Guide* (1909), 186 (no. 669), is erroneous in giving Thebes as the provenance as no provenance is given in the original sale catalogue.

2. Lot 134, Sotheby sale 29 June 1835.

Plates 88–91

Naos of *Pȝ-sȝ-nsw* 1135

Date: New Kingdom
Provenance: Not recorded[1]
Date of acquisition: 1893
Material: Limestone
Dimensions: 75 cm *h.* (without hawk), 15 cm *h.* (hawk), 38 cm *w.*, 39.5 cm *deep*

This naos contains a figure of Osiris inside it and has a hawk on top. Texts are incised around the pedestal on which the naos sits (A, B) and on the front of the naos (C, D) consisting of prayers on behalf of the scribe of offerings of all the gods Pasanesu. The right side of the shrine bears a scene in sunk relief showing Pasanesu offering incense to Osiris (E), while a scene on the left side depicts him worshipping Ptah-Tatenen (F). A scene on the rear of the naos portrays Harsiese in the company of Isis and Nephthys (G). The top of the naos is also inscribed (H). A cartouche, apparently of Amenemhat III, on the top of the naos may relate to the worship of that king since it cannot be regarded as contemporary to his reign, being written with the 𓋔 sign which was commonly used instead of the 𓈖 sign from the New Kingdom.

Preservation and colour: The naos is well preserved apart from several gouges, especially on the corners and left side. The bottom of the pedestal has been damaged and repaired in modern times.

Bibliography: *Sculpture Guide* (1909), 51–2 (no. 174).

1. The provenance of Meidum given in *Sculpture Guide* (1909), 52 (no. 174), is erroneous. No provenance is given in the original documents concerning the purchase and Meidum has probably been deduced only from the cartouche of Amenemhat III.

Plates 92–95

Statue of *Mḥw* and *Dwȝt* 460

Date: Nineteenth Dynasty
Provenance: Not recorded
Date of acquisition: 1839 (Anastasi collection)
Material: Limestone
Dimensions: 62.4 cm *h.*, 41.5 cm *w.*, 33.3 cm *deep*

This fine pair statue of the overseer of construction of Amun in Luxor Mahu and his wife Duat is inscribed with prayers down the front of their figures (A, B), along the bottom of the front and two sides of the statue (C, D), on the sides of the statue (E, F) and on the back (G, H).

Mahu appears to be otherwise unattested.

Preservation and colour: This statue has been cut in two at some time in the past with consequent damage to the opening lines of the two inscriptions (G, H) on the back. The base of the statue is battered and there are gouges elsewhere, resulting in some damage to the texts. The nose of the male figure is slightly damaged. The wigs of the figures are black. The face, hands and feet of Mahu are red-brown, while his collars are red and black. The face of Duat is yellow with red lips, collars and bangles. The eyes of the figures are black. The garments of the figures would appear to have been originally painted white, although this colour has now faded away to reveal the natural stone. There are traces of blue paint on some of the hieroglyphs and red paint on the lines bordering the inscriptions.

Bibliography: Sharpe, *Eg. Inscr.* 2nd ser., pls. 78–9; *Sculpture Guide* (1909), 177 (no. 637); Vandier, *Manuel* III, 442, 651; Helck, *Materialien*, 45.

Plates 96–97

1. Statue of a woman 484

Date: Ramesside
Provenance: Not recorded
Date of acquisition: 1891
Material: Black granite
Dimensions: 44.6 cm *h.*, 28.3 cm *w.*

The upper part of a fine female statue. The lady is wearing an elaborate wig and collar. Two columns of text are incised on the back pillar invoking Hathor and Mut.

Preservation and colour: Only the upper part of the statue remains. The edges where the lower half was broken off are damaged. The nose is battered, and the right side of the wig is slightly chipped.

Bibliography: *Sculpture Guide* (1909), 186 (no. 668); Vandier, *Manuel* III, 439.

2. Stela of *ꜥb-mnw* 1753

Date: New Kingdom
Provenance: Not recorded
Date of acquisition: 1931
Material: Limestone
Dimensions: 29.5 cm *h*., 22.5 cm *w*.

This small, round-topped stela is divided into two registers with incised texts and figures in raised relief. At the top of the upper register is a winged sun-disk, while below is depicted the bark of Amen-Reꜥ with a ram's head at either end. At the front of the bark stand the figures of Tutu and Maat. In the lower register, on the right, the figure of the servant of the table and butcher Abmenu is depicted in raised relief in an attitude of adoration. A line of text above him and six columns of text on the left carry a prayer on his behalf to Amun.

Preservation and colour: The top left corner of the stela is lost and there is a long diagonal gash on the surface. The lower edge is battered and much of the surface of the stela is worn. The stela is disfigured by numerous black smudges.

Bibliography: None.

3. Stela of *Mḥiꜣ* 1471

Date: Ramesside
Provenance: Memphis
Date of acquisition: 1908[1]
Material: Limestone
Dimensions: 22.3 cm *h*., 17.1 cm *w*.

This small, round-topped stela originally had incised on its face forty-four ears divided into six rows on each side of the stela, the top and bottom of which was comprised of three ears and the rest four ears. A column of text down the centre contains a prayer to Ptah, while a line of text at the bottom names the dedicator Mahuia.

Preservation and colour: The stela has lost its upper right-hand corner and its lower left-hand one, both of which have been restored in modern times. The surface is covered with small scratches and some black stains. There are faint traces of red paint in some of the ears.

Bibliography: W. M. F. Petrie, *Memphis* I (London, 1909), 7, 9, pl. XIII, no. 30; *Sculpture Guide* (1909), 304 (no. 1171); Porter and Moss, *Top. Bibl.* III^2, 834.

1. Presented by the Egypt Research Account.

Plates 98–99

Stela of *Mḥw* 1369

Date: Ramesside
Provenance: Not recorded
Date of acquisition: 1902
Material: Limestone
Dimensions: 74.5 cm *h*., 49 cm *w*.

This stela is in the form of a doorway with a cavetto cornice and torus-moulding. A prayer is inscribed on each side of the upper lintel continuing down the jambs – the one on the left to Osiris and the one on the right to Anubis, both on behalf of the overseer of the portal Mahu. There are two scenes in sunk relief on the central area of the doorway. The upper scene depicts Osiris enthroned in a shrine on the left behind an altar of offerings. He is being worshipped on the right side by Mahu and a royal prince with a sidelock holding a floral offering. The name of the prince is largely illegible, apparently *Mry-'Imn(?)-pꜣy*...(?). In the lower scene Mahu is seated on the left with the king's daughter *Nbw-m-tḫy* and the lady *Bꜣkt*. Before them is an altar heaped with offerings. On the right his daughter *Mwt-ꜣḫt* pours a libation over the altar.

The owner and the royal prince cannot be further identified. The princess is presumably to be identified with the Princess Nebuemtekh who is named on vase no. 507 and plaque no. 813 in the Louvre (E. Chassinat, *Revue de l'Égypte Ancienne* 1 (1927), 132) and vases BM 4536 (*Guide* (1922), 18 no. 33), Leiden H 240, H 329, H 330 (B. Stricker, *Oudheidkundige Mededelingen uit het Rijksmuseum van Oudheden te Leiden* 24 (1943), 81–84), Munich ÄS 243 and 247 (*Staatliche Sammlung* Ägyptischer Kunst, 2nd ed., (1976), 197) and Turin 3247–8 (A. Fabretti, F. Rossi and R. V. Lanzone, *Regio Museo di Torino* (Turin, 1882), 442–3; G. Maspero, *Rec. trav.* 4 (1883), 151, no. xviii; H. Gauthier, *Rec. trav.* 40 (1923), 202, no. 32). Chassinat wrongly dated the princess to the Middle Kingdom, while Stricker and the Munich catalogue correctly assign the vases to the New Kingdom. The paternity of the princess remains unknown.

Preservation and colour: The stela is much battered along the edges. The upper scene is very worn and discoloured in places. The upper edge on the right side of the scene is so damaged that the hieroglyphs are barely visible. There are two drilled holes, one on the right and the other on the left of the underside of the lintel, and corresponding holes on the upper surface of the base. These were not drilled very deep in the stone and possibly were intended as supports for wooden doors.

Bibliography: *Sculpture Guide* (1909), 188 (no. 678).

Plates 100–101

1. Stela of *Ḥꜣtiꜣ* 772

Date: New Kingdom
Provenance: Not recorded
Date of acquisition: 1850
Material: Limestone
Dimensions: 57.5 cm *h*., 40 cm *w*.

This round-topped stela is divided into three registers with figures in sunk relief and incised texts. In the upper register Hatia on the right pours a libation over an altar heaped with offerings. Behind it Osiris is enthroned in the centre of the register. Isis and Horus stand behind him. In the second register the lady *Mꜥy* is seated on the left behind an altar piled with offerings. Hatia pours a libation over this altar accompanied by the lady *Sꜣt-iry*. *Ptḥ-pꜣy* and the lady *Br* are seated on the right behind an altar heaped with offerings.

In the third register *P3-šdy* is seated on the left behind an altar covered with offerings over which a libation is poured by *Stḫ-ms* followed by the lady *B3k(t)-'Imn*. On the right sits the lady *T3-mḥy(t)*, to whom offerings are being made by the lady *Ḥtp* and *'Imn-m-ḥb*.

Preservation and colour: The stela is much damaged and worn along the edges and corners. It is discoloured by brown stains and is suffering badly from salt which is lifting the surface in places.

Bibliography: *Sculpture Guide* (1909), 201 (no. 730).

2. Stela of *Ḥwy* 1745

Date: New Kingdom
Provenance: Not recorded
Date of acquisition: 1931
Material: Limestone
Dimensions: 35 cm *h*., 23.2 cm *w*.

This round-topped stela is divided into three registers with incised texts and figures in sunk relief. In the upper section there is a Hathor head in the centre flanked by a cat on each side. In the middle register on the left the goddess Mut is enthroned in a kiosk on a bark being worshipped by the hall-keeper of Amun Huy who kneels on the right. Below in the third register stand three male and two female figures before an altar heaped with offerings on the extreme left. They are named as *Rs*, *Nfr-ḥtp*, *...y*(?), *(T)wy*(?) and *Mwt-m-(i)pt*.

These individuals cannot be further identified.

Preservation and colour: The stela is not in the best state of preservation. The surface is worn and broken in many places and covered in black blotches. The edges of the stela are battered in several places.

Bibliography: None.

Plates 102–103

1. Stela of *Ḥwy* 364

Date: Eighteenth–Nineteenth Dynasty
Provenance: Not recorded
Date of acquisition: 1839 (Anastasi collection)
Material: Limestone
Dimensions: 50.5 cm *h*., 31.5 cm *w*.

Two registers with figures in sunk relief and incised texts occupy the face of this stela. In the upper register Osiris is seated on the left and before him stands the altar-porter of the temple of Ptah Huy, holding floral offerings. He is followed by his son *'Imn-m-ipt* and his daughter *Py*, also carrying offerings.

In the lower register Huy and his wife *Kfn3* are seated on the left. Beside them stands a small child, their son *Mniw*. On the right three of Huy's children stand with offerings: his daughter *Nky*(?), his daughter *T3-wsrt* and his son *Mr-n-Ptḥ*.

The title of Huy might indicate that he held office in Memphis in which case this stela could originate from Saqqara.

Preservation and colour: This stela is worn in parts, especially at the bottom. There are several scratches and a large gouge across the surface. There are traces of red paint on the neck of Osiris and the feet of Merenptah.

Bibliography: Lieblein, *Dictionnaire*, no. 862; *Sculpture Guide* (1909), 219 (no. 792); Helck, *Materialien*, 135.

2. Stela of *'Imn-ms* 323

Date: Ramesside
Provenance: Abydos
Date of acquisition: 1837 (Athanasi collection)[1]
Material: Limestone
Dimensions: 42.7 cm *h*., 26 cm *w*.

There is a large, Hathor-headed sistrum in the centre of this round-topped stela flanked by lotus flowers around the head. In the lower right-hand corner the sculptor of Amun, Amenmose, stands in adoration holding a brazier. On the left the lady *B3k(t)-Stḫ* stands with her arms raised in worship.

These individuals are otherwise unknown.

Preservation and colour: There are several gouges and areas of wear on the surface of the stela and the edges are damaged in places. The wear on the face of the Seth animal may not necessarily be intentional.

Bibliography: *Sculpture Guide* (1909), 204–5 (no. 744).

1. Lot 697, Sotheby sale 13 March 1837.

Index to Numbers

No.	*Plate*	*No.*	*Plate*	*No.*	*Plate*
107	22–23	460	92–95	1632	82–83
142	22–23	472	66–67	1654	20–21
153	56–57	474	74–77	1725	82–83
264	32–33	484	96–97	1726	24–27
266	46–47	547	44–45	1745	100–101
269	30–31	549	62–63	1753	96–97
270	54–55	555	30–31	1784	16–17
271	38–39	646	68–69	1831	84–85
277	54–55	697	4–7	2559	28–29
279	50–51	700	70–71	12247	48–49
284	36–37	772	100–101	29282	10–11
286	40–41	796	72–73	29951	14–15
288	58–59	811	52–53	29952	14–15
292	58–59	812	52–53	32623	2–3
309	60–61	814	36–37	49234	8–9
321	70–71	816	34–35	54420	14–15
323	102–103	853	78–79	58468b	1
332	46–47	891	80–81	58468d	1
341	32–33	1135	88–91	63783	42–43
349	60–61	1184	84–85	65593	28–29
350	64–65	1198	24–25	66667	20–21
351	66–67	1231	12–13	66668	18–19
364	102–103	1347	38–39	68173	14–15
371	34–35	1369	98–99	68675	12–13
374	50–51	1382	86–87	69089	44–45
446	40–41	1430	80–81		
455	68–69	1471	96–97		

Indexes of Names and Titles

1 Royal Names

Ahmes-Nefertari 277 (pls. 54–55), 446 (pls. 40–41), 811 (pls. 52–53), 1347 (pls. 38–39)
Amenemhat III 1135 (pls. 90–91)
Amenhotep I 153 (pls. 56–57), 277 (pls. 54–55), 446 (pls. 40–41), 811 (pls. 52–53), 1347 (pls. 38–39)
Bintanat 697 (pls. 4–5)
Horemheb 58468b (pl. 1), 58468d (pl. 1)
Ramesses II 142 (pls. 22–23), 697 (pls. 4–7), 1231 (pls. 12–13), 1726 (pls. 26–27), 29282 (pls. 10–11), 49234 (pls. 8–9), 68675 (pls. 12–13)
Ramesses III 1198 (pls. 24–25), 1784 (pls. 16–17), 66667 (pls. 20–21)
Ramesses IV 54420 (pls. 14–15), 66668 (pls. 18–19)
Ramesses VI 68173 (pls. 14–15)
Sety I 32623 (pls. 2–3)
Tausret 22951 (pls. 14–15), 29952 (pls. 14–15)
Thutmose III 153 (pls. 56–57)

2 Private Names

ꜣny m. 796 (pls. 72–73)
ꜣst f. 349 (pls. 60–61)
ꜣst-wrt f. 292 (pls. 58–59)
ꜣšꜣmriꜣ m. 1382 (pls. 86–87)

'Iꜣ m. 292 (pls. 58–59)
'Ii f. 371 (pls. 34–35)
'Iiꜣ m. 69089 (pls. 44–45)
'Iim m. 288 (pls. 58–59)
'Iwnꜣiꜣ m. 351(2) (pls. 66–67)
'Iwnw m. 351 (pls. 66–67)
'Ibwdb m. 309 (pls. 60–61)
'Ifm (?) f. 371 (pls. 34–35)
'Ipy 321 (pls. 70–71), 332 (pls. 46–47)
'Imn-m-ipt m. 349 (pls. 60–61), 364 (pls. 102–103), 816 (pls. 34–35)
'Imn-m-wiꜣ m. 351 (pls. 66–67)
'Imn-m-ḥb m. 474 (pls. 74–77), 772 (pls. 100–101)
'Imn-ms m. 107 (pls. 22–23), 142 (pls. 22–23), 323 (pls. 102–103), 351 (pls. 66–67), 1632 (pls. 82–83), 1654 (pls. 20–21)
'Imn-nḫt m. 374 (pls. 50–51)
'Imn-ḫꜥ m. 349 (pls. 60–61)
'Inihꜣy f. 349 (pls. 60–61)
'Iry-nfr m. 284 (pls. 36–37), 814 (pls. 36–37)
'It-n-it.f m. 279 (pls. 50–51)

ꜥꜣ(t)-niwt f. 321 (pls. 70–71)
ꜥb-pdt m. 1831 (pls. 84–85)
ꜥb-mnw m. 1753 (pls. 96–97)
ꜥn-Mwt f. 549 (pls. 62–63)
ꜥnḳt-m-ḥb f. 292 (pls. 58–59)

Wp-wꜣwt-ms m. 1184 (pls. 84–85)
Wrt-wꜣḥ-sw f. 349 (pls. 60–61)
Wrt-nfrt f. 549 (pls. 62–63)
Wrnr f. 474 (pls. 76–77), 547 (pls. 44–45), 1347 (pls. 38–39)
Wsr-mꜣꜥt-rꜥ-nḫt m. 292 (pls. 58–59)
Wsr-ḥꜣt m. 1184 (pls. 84–85)

Bꜣk m. 12247 (pls. 48–49)
Bꜣk-ꜥꜣ m. 321 (pls. 70–71)
Bꜣk-n-'Imn m. 349 (pls. 60–61)
Bꜣk-n-wrn(r) m. 549 (pls. 62–63)
Bꜣk-n-Mwt m. 549 (pls. 62–63), 1347 (pls. 38–39)
Bꜣkt f. 1369 (pls. 98–99)
Bꜣkt-'Imn f. 351 (pls. 66–67), 772 (pls. 100–101)
Bꜣk(t)-wrn(r) f. 474 (pls. 74–75)
Bꜣkt-Ptḥ f. 309 (pls. 60–61)
Bꜣk(t)-Mwt f. 288(2) (pls. 58–59)
Bꜣk(t)-Stḫ f. 323 (pls. 102–103)
Br f. 772 (pls. 100–101)

Pꜣ-pr-ꜥꜣ-(r)-nḥḥ m. 350 (pls. 64–65)
Pꜣ-mr-iḥw m. 292 (pls. 58–59), 853 (pls. 78–79)
P(ꜣ)-n-ꜥImn m. 309 (pls. 60–61)
P(ꜣ)-n-nw (?) m. 341 (pls. 32–33)
P(ꜣ)-n-nfrw m. 812 (pls. 52–53)
P(ꜣ)-n-Rꜥ m. 1784 (pls. 16–17)
P(ꜣ)-n-rnw m. 796 (pls. 72–73)
P(ꜣ)-n-grw m. 288(2) (pls. 58–59)
P(ꜣ)-n-Tꜣ-wrt m. 811 (pls. 52–53), 1184 (pls. 84–85), 1632 (pls. 82–83)
Pꜣ-nfr m. 549 (pls. 62–63)
Pꜣ-[nḫt] m. 63783 (pls. 42–43)
Pꜣ-nḫt-m-ṯ (?) m. 796 (pls. 72–73)
Pꜣ-Rꜥ-m-ḥb m. 349 (pls. 60–61)
Pꜣ-rn-nfr m. 271 (pls. 38–39), 1347 (pls. 38–39)
Pꜣ-sꜣ-nsw m. 1135 (pls. 88–91)
Pꜣ-sr 349 (pls. 60–61), 1784 (pls. 16–17)
Pꜣ-šd m. 264 (pls. 32–33), 341 (pls. 32–33)
Pꜣ-šdy m. 772 (pls. 100–101)
Pꜣ-tꜣ (?) m. 321 (pls. 70–71)
Pꜣ-tꜣ-ḥrr m. 292 (pls. 58–59)
Py f. 364 (pls. 102–103)
Pyiꜣy m. 1725 (pls. 82–83)
Ptrm (?) m. 350 (pls. 64–65)
Ptḥ. . . m. 549 (pls. 62–63)
Ptḥ-pꜣ. . . m. 549 (pls. 62–63)
Ptḥ-pꜣy m. 772 (pls. 100–101)
Ptḥ-(m)-wiꜣ m. 350 (pls. 64–65)
Ptḥ-m-ḥb m. 796 (pls. 72–73)
Ptḥ-ms m. 288 (pls. 58–59)
Ptḥ-nḫt m. 288 (pls. 58–59)

Mꜣꜣ-nḫt.f m. 269 (pls. 30–31)
Mꜥy f. 772 (pls. 100–101)
Mwt-ꜣḫt f. 1369 (pls. 98–99)
Mwt-m-ꜥIwnw f. 349 (pls. 60–61)
Mwt-m-(i)pt f. 1745 (pls. 100–101)
Mwt-m-int f. 1198 (pls. 24–25)
Mwt-m-wiꜣ f. 288 (pls. 58–59), 351 (pls. 66–67), 1347 (pls. 38–39)
Mwt-m-wsḫt f. 288 (pls. 58–59), 309(2) (pls. 60–61)
Mniw m. 364 (pls. 102–103)
Mr-Ptḥ-(m)-pr-'Imn m. 350 (pls. 64–65)
Mr-mšꜥ.f m. 350 (pls. 64–65)
Mr-n-Ptḥ m. 364 (pls. 102–103)
Mry f. 321 (pls. 70–71), 371 (pls. 34–35)
Mry-'Imn-pꜣy. . . (?) m. 1369 (pls. 98–99)
Mryt-Ptḥ f. 288(2) (pls. 58–59)
Ms m. 549 (pls. 62–63)
Mḥiꜣ m. 1471 (pls. 96–97)
Mḥy m. 351 (pls. 66–67)
Mḥy(t)-ḫꜥ.ti f. 284 (pls. 36–37)
Mḥw m. 460 (pls. 92–95), 1369 (pls. 98–99), 1654 (pls. 20–21)
Mtr f. 350 (pls. 64–65)

Nꜣiꜣ f. 288 (pls. 58–59)
Nꜣ-ḥr-ḥr m. 309 (pls. 60–61)
Nb-'Imn m. 474 (pls. 74–75)
Nb-nfr m. 811 (pls. 52–53), 1184 (pls. 84–85)
Nbt-tꜣwy f. 1184 (pls. 84–85)
Nbw-m-tḫy f. 1369 (pls. 98–99)

Nfr f. 279 (pls. 50–51)
Nfr-ꜥbw 269 (pls. 30–31), 2559 (pls. 28–29), 65593 (pls. 28–29)
Nfr-m-mr.s(t) f. 371 (pls. 34–35)
Nfr-rnpt m. 288 (pls. 58–59), 796(2) (pls. 72–73)
Nfr-ḥtp m. 1745 (pls. 100–101)
Nfrt-ii.ti f. 446 (pls. 40–41), 547 (pls. 44–45)
Nfrt-iry f. 107 (pls. 22–23), 142 (pls. 22–23), 309 (pls. 60–61), 349 (pls. 60–61)
Ns-ʾImn m. 292 (pls. 58–59)
Ns-Rꜥ m. 292 (pls. 58–59)
Nhy f. 309 (pls. 60–61)
Nhyhꜣy f. 547 (pls. 44–45)
Nhrti m. 474 (pls. 74–75)
Nḫt-ʾImn m. 371 (pls. 34–35)
Nḫt-m-Wꜣst m. 796 (pls. 72–73)
Nḫt-Mnw m. 292(2) (pls. 58–59)
Nky f. 364 (pls. 102–103)

Rꜥ-(m)-wiꜣ m. 351 (pls. 66–67)
Rꜥ-ms m. 107 (pls. 22–23), 142 (pls. 22–23), 288 (pls. 58–59)
Rꜥ-mss-m-pr-ʾItm m. 350 (pls. 64–65)
Rꜥ-ms-sw-m-pr-Rꜥ m. 796 (pls. 72–73)
Rnw(t) f. 288 (pls. 58–59)
Rs m. 1745 (pls. 100–101)

Ḥꜣti m. 1726 (pls. 24–27)
Ḥꜣtiꜣ m. 772 (pls. 100–101)
Ḥꜥp-ꜥꜣ m. 1184 (pls. 84–85)
Ḥwy m. 288(2) (pls. 58–59), 349 (pls. 60–61), 364 (pls. 102–103), 446 (pls. 40–41), 1745 (pls. 100–101)
Ḥwt-ii f. 811 (pls. 52–53)
Ḥwt-ḥr f. 796 (pls. 72–73), 1184 (pls. 84–85), 1654 (pls. 20–21), 1725 (pls. 82–83)
Ḥpt-di-sw (?) f. 1184 (pls. 84–85)
Ḥnwt-mtr f. 549 (pls. 62–63)
Ḥnwt-nfrt f. 309 (pls. 60–61)
Ḥnwt-tꜣ-nb f. 700 (pls. 70–71)
Ḥnr f. 549 (pls. 62–63)
Ḥr-m-ḥꜣt m. 796 (pls. 72–73)
Ḥr-mnw m. 321 (pls. 70–71)
Ḥr-ms m. 66667 (pls. 20–21)
Ḥr.s f. 371 (pls. 34–35)
Ḥri m. 891 (pls. 80–81), 1430 (pls. 80–81), 1784 (pls. 16–17), 66667 (pls. 20–21), 66668 (pls. 18–19)
Ḥtp f. 772 (pls. 100–101)

Ḫꜣr m. 549 (pls. 62–63)
Ḫꜥ-bḫnt m. 555 (pls. 30–31)
Ḫꜥ-m-ipt m. 472 (pls. 66–67)
Ḫꜥt-bꜣḫt f. 349 (pls. 60–61)
Ḫnsw m. 796(2) (pls. 72–73), 1430 (pls. 80–81)

Sꜣiꜣ f. 1184 (pls. 84–85)
Sꜣt-iry f. 772 (pls. 100–101)
Sꜣḥti f. 555 (pls. 30–31)
Swr m. 796 (pls. 72–73)
Swty-ms m. 796 (pls. 72–73)
Sbꜣ m. 446 (pls. 40–41)
Smn-tꜣwy m. 279 (pls. 50–51)
Sḫmt f. 1184 (pls. 84–85)
Stḫ-ms m. 772 (pls. 100–101)
Stḫ-nḫt m. 1831 (pls. 84–85)

Šrit-Rꜥ f. 1347 (pls. 38–39)

Ḳꜣy-tꜣ-nḫb(t) f. 292 (pls. 58–59)
Ḳꜣḥꜣ m. 69089 (pls. 44–45)
Ḳn-ḥr-ḫpš.f m. 63783 (pls. 42–43)

Kfnꜣ f. 364 (pls. 102–103)
Kmꜥ m. 66668 (pls. 18–19)

Tꜣ-ʾIwnw f. 279 (pls. 50–51)
Tꜣ-n(t)-ḥr-twy-st (?) f. 292 (pls. 58–59)
Tꜣ-ꜥḳy f. 1831 (pls. 84–85)
Tꜣ-wrt f. 1184 (pls. 84–85), 1430 (pls. 80–81)
Tꜣ-wrt-m-mḥ (?) f. 811 (pls. 52–53)
Tꜣ-wrt-ḥtp.ti f. 309 (pls. 60–61), 549 (pls. 62–63)
Tꜣ-wsrt f. 364 (pls. 102–103)
Tꜣ-mi(t) f. 288 (pls. 58–59)
Tꜣ-mḥyt f. 772 (pls. 100–101)
Tꜣ-nfrt f. 474 (pls. 74–77)
Tꜣ-nḥs f. 288 (pls. 58–59)
Tꜣ-rnw f. 549 (pls. 62–63)
Tꜣ-ḥꜣr f. 446 (pls. 40–41)
Tꜣ-kꜣri f. 288 (pls. 58–59)
Tꜣ-kꜣrt f. 349 (pls. 60–61)
Tꜣ-ṯhrt f. 549 (pls. 62–63)
Tꜣy f. 288 (pls. 58–59)
Tꜣy-bs f. 1831 (pls. 84–85)
Tꜣ...nbt f. 1347 (pls. 38–39)
Tyiꜣy f. 351 (pls. 66–67)
Twy f. 309(3) (pls. 60–61), 351 (pls. 66–67), 1745 (pls. 100–101), 69089 (pls. 44–45)
Twnn-nḫb-Ḫnsw m. 700 (pls. 70–71)
Tnt-ʾImntt f. 69089 (pls. 44–45)

Dwꜣ-m-mr.st f. 446 (pls. 40–41)
Dwꜣt f. 460 (pls. 92–95)
Ḏḥwty-ḥr-mkt.f m. 266 (pls. 46–47), 547 (pls. 44–45)

...i f. 1745 (pls. 100–101)
...pꜣ-ḥꜥp m. 371 (pls. 34–35)
...Mwt f. 351 (pls. 66–67)

3 Titles

ꜣṯw 1831 (pls. 84–5)

imy-r pr n ḥwt Rꜥ-mss mry-ʾImn 1726 (pls. 26–27)
imy-r pr n ḥwt-nṯr Rꜥ-ms-sw mry-ʾImn ꜥn ẖr ḥb sdw mi Ptḥ-Tꜣ-ṯnn 142 (pls. 22–23)
imy-r pr n ḥwt-nṯr Rꜥ-ms-sw mry-ʾImn ꜥn ẖr ḥb sdw mrt mi Ptḥ-Tꜣ-ṯnn 142 (pls. 22–23)
imy-r mšꜥ 853 (pls. 78–79)
imy-r mšꜥ wr 853 (pls. 78–79)
imy-r nww n ʾImn 107 (pls. 22–23), 142 (pls. 22–23)
imy-r nww n ʾImn-Rꜥ 142 (pls. 22–23)
imy-r rwyt 1369 (pls. 98–99)
imy-r ḫꜣswt nbw n ʾImn-Rꜥ nsw nṯrw 1784 (pls. 16–17)
imy-r ḫꜣswt rsywt 66667 (pls. 20–21)
imy-r kꜣwt n ʾImn 460 (pls. 92–95)
imy-r kꜣwt n ʾImn m ʾIpt-Swt 460 (pls. 94–95)
imy-r kꜣwt n ʾImn m ʾIpt rsyt 460 (pls. 92–95)
ir wꜣt šwy n tꜣ wꜥbt n pr ꜥꜣ 549 (pls. 62–63)
iry ꜥt n ʾImn 1745 (pls. 100–101)
iry wsḫt ḥm.f 142 (pls. 22–23)
it nṯr n Rꜥ-ʾItm m pr-ꜥnḫ 309 (pls. 60–61)
idnw wꜣt šwy 549 (pls. 62–63)
idnw n ḥwt Rꜥ-ms-sw mry-ʾImn m wiꜣ...pr ʾInḥr 1726 (pls. 26–27)
idnw n Kš 1784 (pls. 16–17)

wꜥb 292 (pls. 58–59), 349 (pls. 60–61), 351 (pls. 66–67), 1632 (pls. 82–83)
wꜥb ꜥwy 351 (pls. 66–67)
wꜥb n ʾImn 700 (pls. 70–71), 1632 (pls. 82–83)
wꜥb n ʾImn n ꜥt irp 349 (pls. 60–61)
wꜥb (n) pr-Rꜥ-Ḥr-ꜣḫty 292 (pls. 58–59)
wꜥrtw see ꜣṯw
wbꜣ n ṯꜣt 1753 (pls. 96–97)
wbs (?) 350 (pls. 64–65)
wnmy wr 107 (pls. 22–23)
wnmy wr n nb tꜣwy 142 (pls. 22–23)
wr diw 1831 (pls. 84–85)
wḥm nsw m-bꜣḥ tmw iw ḥm.f ḫꜥw 142 (pls. 22–23)
wdpw n tꜣw 142 (pls. 22–23)

mniw 1184 (pls. 84–85)

nbt pr 279 (pls. 50–51), 284 (pls. 36–37), 288 (pls. 58–59), 309 (pls. 60–61), 321 (pls. 70–71), 323 (pls. 102–103), 349

(pls. 60–61), 371 (pls. 34–35), 446 (pls. 40–41), 460 (pls. 92–95), 474 (pls. 74–77), 555 (pls. 30–31), 700 (pls. 70–71), 772 (pls. 100–101), 811 (pls. 52–53), 1184 (pls. 84–85), 1347 (pls. 38–39), 1369 (pls. 98–99), 1430 (pls. 80–81), 1654 (pls. 20–21), 1725 (pls. 82–83), 69089 (pls. 44–45)
nbt pr.f 292 (pls. 58–59)

ḥꜣty-ꜥ n Bhn 66667 (pls. 20–21)
ḥmt nsw wrt 697 (pls. 4–5)
ḥry iḥw 321 (pls. 70–71)
ḥry iḥw n nb tꜣwy 1430 (pls. 80–81)
ḥry wꜥw n pꜣn (?) 292 (pls. 58–59)
ḥry mnš 321 (pls. 70–71)
ḥry ms wdnw n 'Imn 1382 (pls. 86–87)
ḥry sꜣwty 288 (pls. 58–59), 796 (pls. 72–73)
ḥry sꜣwty nt ḥwt Wsr-mꜣꜥt-rꜥ stp-n-rꜥ m pr 'Imn 796 (pls. 72–73)
ḥry šmsw n ḥm.f 1184 (pls. 84–85)
ḥry kꜣwt n 'Imn 460 (pls. 92–93)
ḥsy ꜥꜣ n nṯr nfr 1632 (pls. 82–83)
ḥsy n nṯr.f 460 (pls. 94–95)
ḥsy(t) n nb tꜣwy 1347 (pls. 38–39)
ḥsyt n Ḥwt.ḥr 460 (pls. 92–93)

ẖry-ꜥ sbꜣ n nb.f 1784 (pls. 16–17)
ẖry-ḥb m pr-nfr 309 (pls. 60–61)
ẖrty nṯr 69089 (pls. 44–45)
ẖrty nṯr n Ḏḥwty nb H̱mnw 266 (pls. 46–47)
ẖtẖt 321 (pls. 70–71)

sꜣ nsw 1369 (pls. 98–99)
sꜣ nsw n Kš 1784 (pls. 16–17), 66667 (pls. 20–21), 66668 (pls. 18–19)
sꜣt nsw 697 (pls. 4–5), 1369 (pls. 98–99)
sꜣwty 288 (pls. 58–59)
sꜣwty n st mꜣꜥt 279 (pls. 50–51)
sꜣwty n st mꜣꜥt ḥr 'Imntt [Wꜣst] 812 (pls. 52–53)
sꜣwty sšw 288 (pls. 58–59)
sꜣb 107 (pls. 22–23), 350 (pls. 64–65), 351 (pls. 66–67)
sft 1753 (pls. 96–97)
sš 288 (pls. 58–59), 309 (pls. 60–61), 351 (pls. 66–67), 1654 (pls. 20–21)
sš wḏḥw 472 (pls. 66–67)
sš wḏḥw n ꜥt irp 349 (pls. 60–61)
sš wḏḥw n nb tꜣwy 107 (pls. 22–23), 472 (pls. 66–67)
sš pr-ḥḏ 1654 (pls. 20–21)
sš mꜣꜥt mry 66667 (pls. 20–21)
sš mšꜥ n nb tꜣwy 474 (pls. 75–77)
sš mḏꜣt nṯr 309 (pls. 60–61)
sš n pꜣ wḏꜣ wꜥb (pls. 66–67)
sš n mšꜥ 292 (pls. 58–59)
sš n st mꜣꜥt 374 (pls. 50–51)
sš n tꜣ st nꜣ šꜥw 288 (pls. 58–59)
sš nfrw 474 (pls. 74–75)
sš nsw 309 (pls. 60–61), 351 (pls. 66–67), 853 (pls. 78–79), 1784 (pls. 16–17), 1831 (pls. 84–85), 63783 (pls. 42–43)
sš nsw wḏḥw n nb tꜣwy 142 (pls. 22–23)
sš nsw mꜣꜥ mr.f 63783 (pls. 42–43)
sš nsw (n) pr-ḥḏ n nb tꜣwy 1430 (pls. 80–81)
sš nṯr 309 (pls. 60–61)
sš ḥwt-nṯr n 'Inḥr 1726 (pls. 24–25)
sš ḥwt-nṯr m pr 'Inḥr 1726 (pls. 26–27)
sš ḥtp(w) n nṯrw nbw 1135 (pls. 88–91)
sš ḳdwt n 'Imn 269 (pls. 30–31), 371 (pls. 34–35)
skt n tꜣ iwꜥyt 891 (pls. 80–81)
skt n tꜣ iwꜥyt (n) pr-ꜥꜣ 891 (pls. 80–81)
sḏꜣwty nṯr 309 (pls. 60–61)
sḏm ꜥš 349 (pls. 60–61), 12247 (pls. 48–49)
sḏm ꜥš m st mꜣꜥt 266 (pls. 46–47), 269 (pls. 30–31), 271 (pls. 38–39), 284 (pls. 36–37), 286 (pls. 40–41), 332 (pls. 46–47), 341 (pls. 32–33), 371 (pls. 34–35), 446 (pls. 40–41), 547 (pls. 44–45), 555 (pls. 30–31), 811 (pls. 52–53), 814 (pls. 36–37), 816 (pls. 34–35), 1347 (pls. 38–39), 12247 (pls. 48–49), 65593 (pls. 28–29), 69089 (pls. 44–45)
sḏm ꜥš m st mꜣꜥt ḥr 'Imntt Wꜣst 264 (pls. 32–33), 266 (pls. 46–47), 269 (pls. 30–31), 1347 (pls. 38–39)
sḏm ꜥš n ṯꜣt 1753 (pls. 96–97)

šmꜥyt 349 (pls. 60–61)
šmꜥyt n(t) 'Imn 107 (pls. 22–23), 288 (pls. 58–59), 349 (pls. 60–61), 351 (pls. 66–67), 460 (pls. 92–95), 474 (pls. 74–75), 549 (pls. 62–63), 700 (pls. 70–71), 1654 (pls. 20–21)
šmꜥyt n(t) 'Imn, Mwt, H̱nsw 1198 (pls. 24–25)
šmꜥyt n(t) 'Imn-Rꜥ 292 (pls. 58–59)
šmꜥyt n(t) Wp-wꜣwt 1184 (pls. 84–85)
šmꜥyt n(t) Mnṯw 474 (pls. 74–75)
šmꜥyt n(t) nbt nht 142 (pls. 22–23), 309 (pls. 60–61)
šmꜥyt n(t) Ḏḥwty 1831 (pls. 84–85)
šmsw 321 (pls. 70–71)

kꜣwty ḥtp pr Ptḥ 364 (pls. 102–103)
kꜣwty ḥtp n Ptḥ 364 (pls. 102–103)
kḏn 1654 (pls. 20–21)

ṯꜣy bs(nt) 700 (pls. 70–71)
ṯꜣy n 'Imn 323 (pls. 102–103)
ṯꜣy ẖw ḥr wnm nsw 66667 (pls. 20–21)
ṯꜣy sryt 279 (pls. 50–51)

Plates

A Note on the Drawings

Damaged areas of text only are marked with cross-hatching; damaged areas of representations are shown as blank.

Colour is indicated only when it adds significantly to the outline and design; black paint is indicated as a solid area of ink.

Not to scale

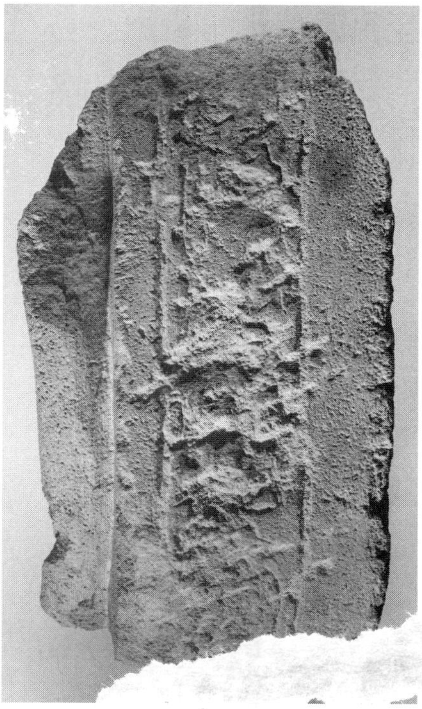

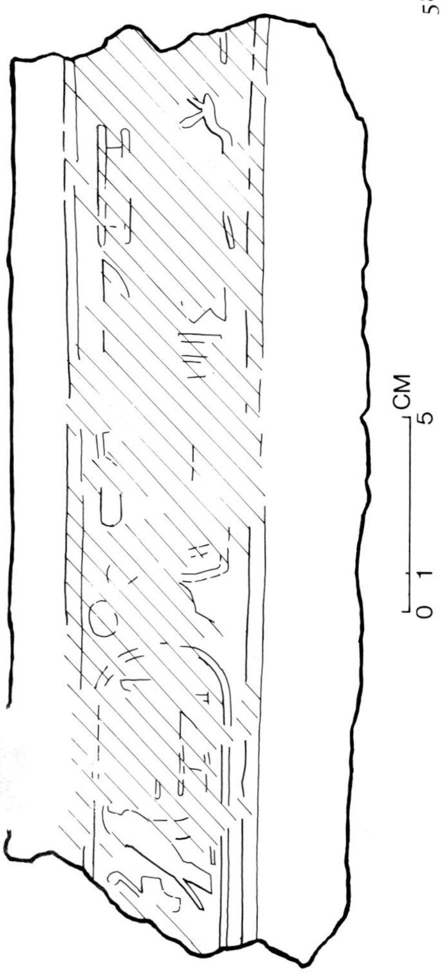

58468d

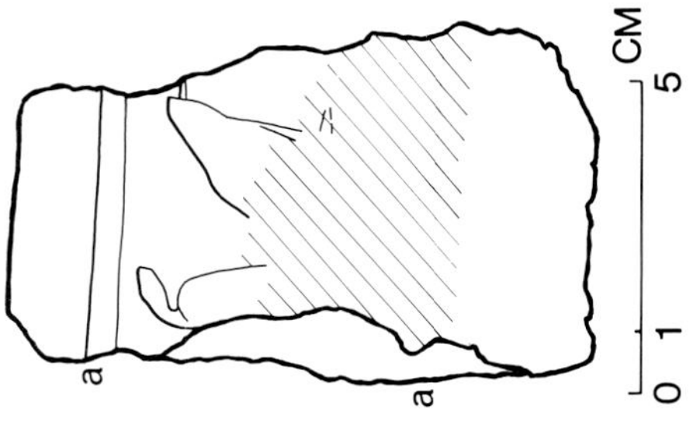

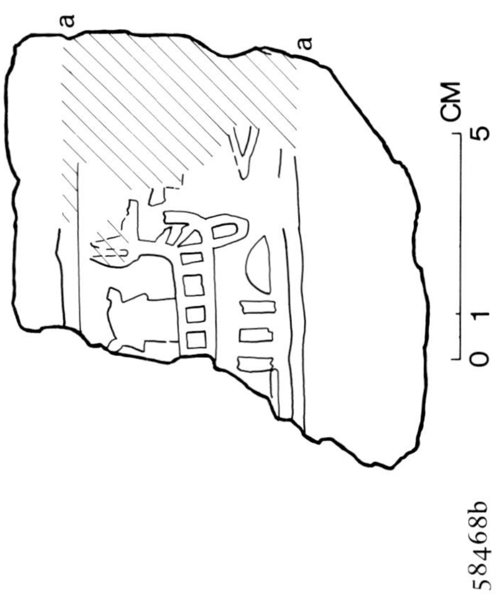

58468b

PLATE 2

Not to scale

32623

32623

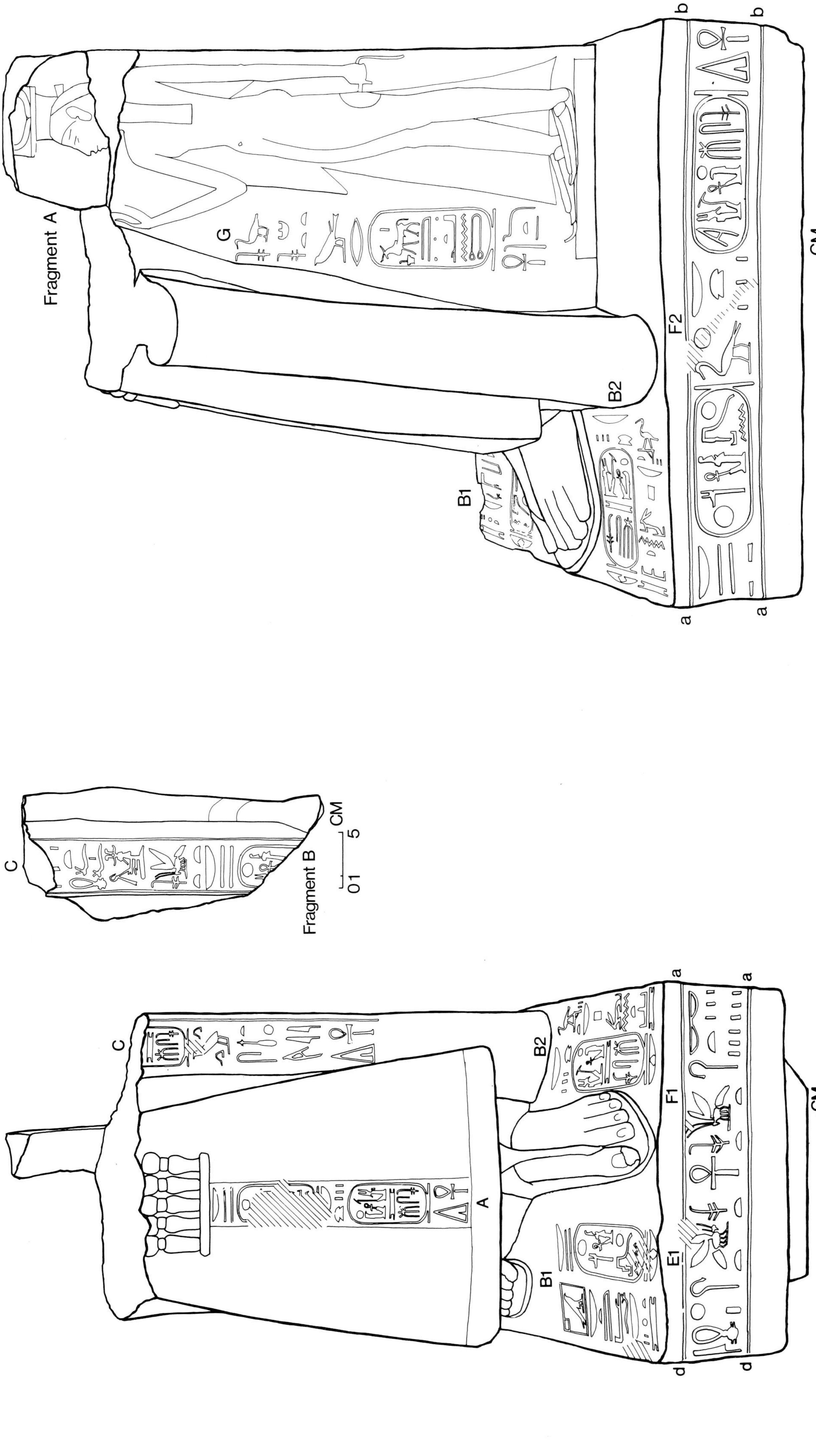
Fragment A
G
B1
B2
F2
a
b
CM
Fragment B
C
A
F1
E1
d

697

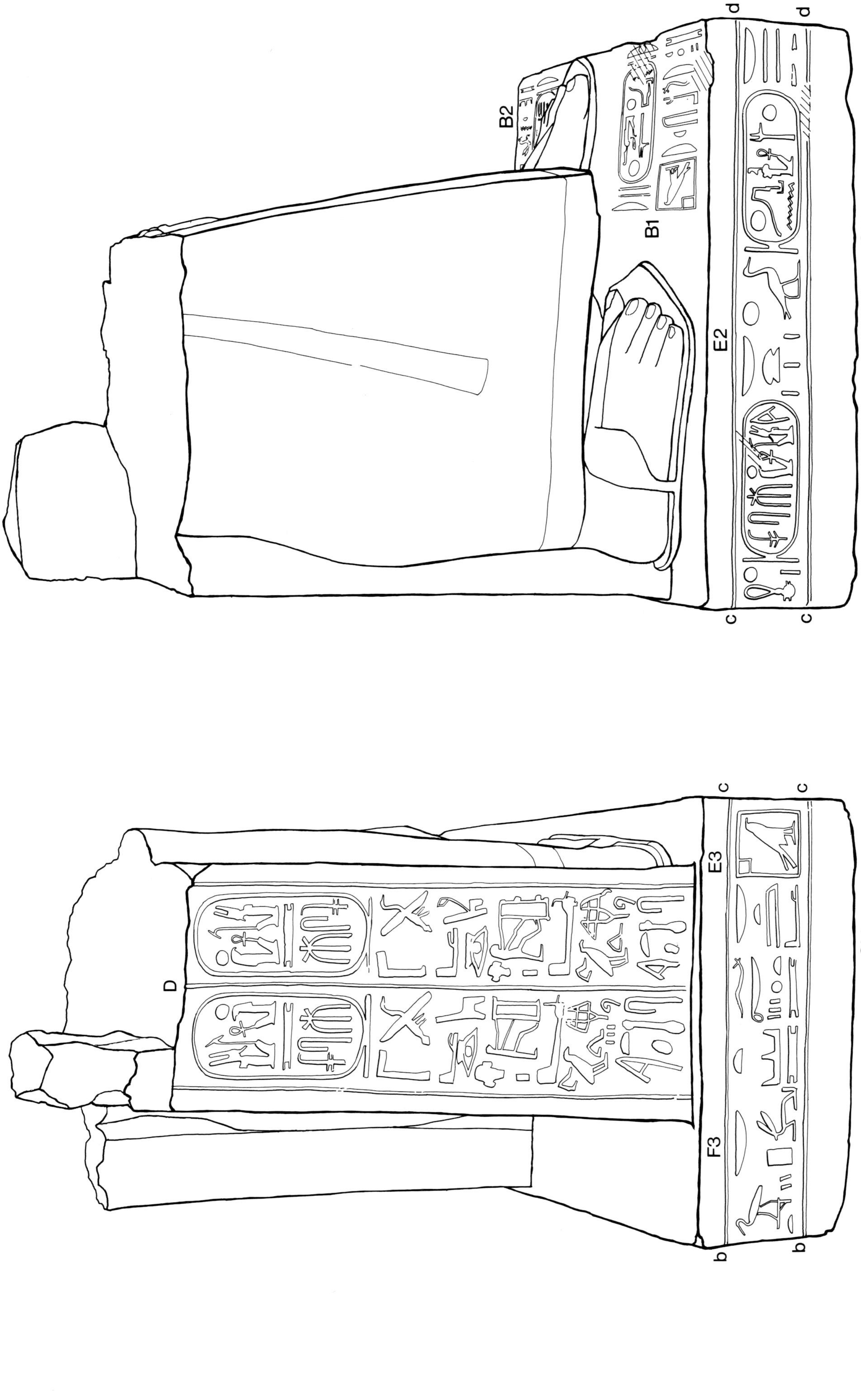

697

PLATE 8

49234

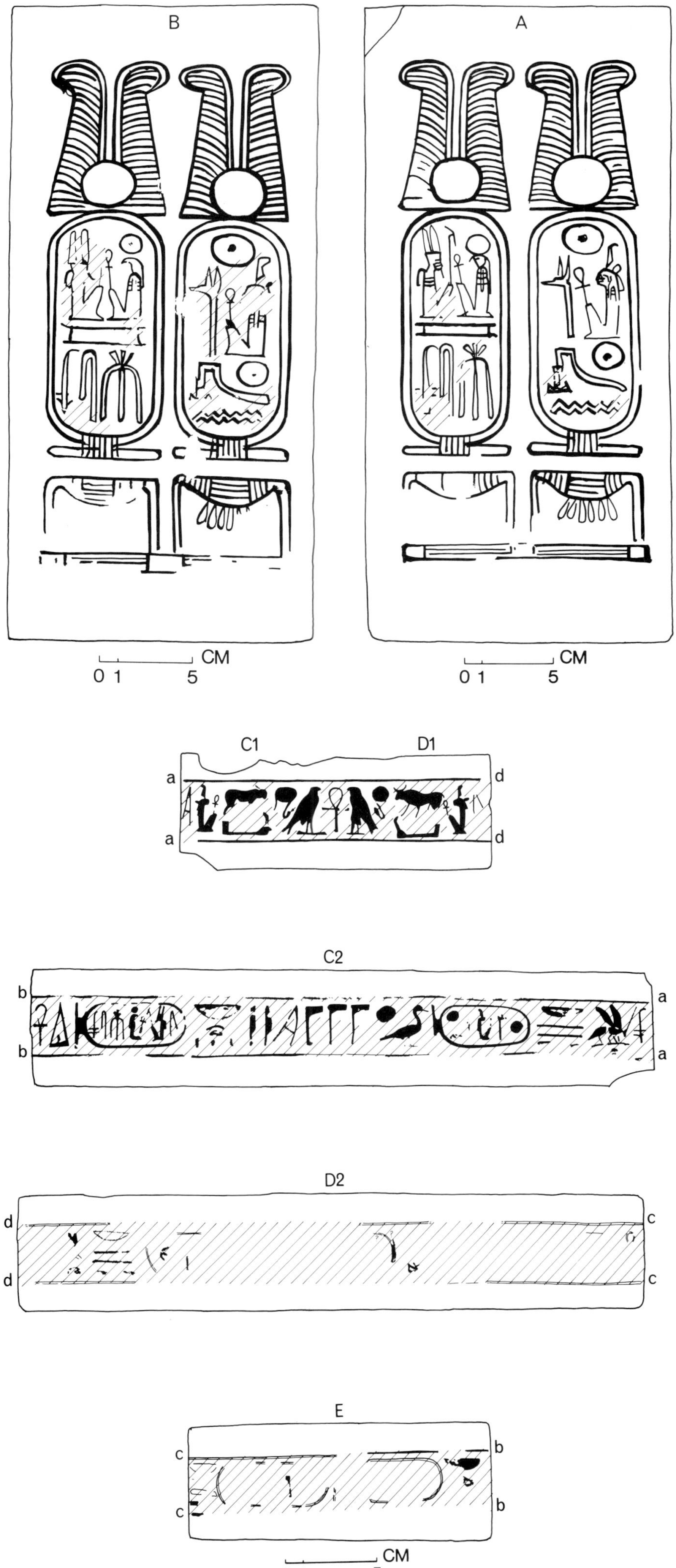

49234

29282

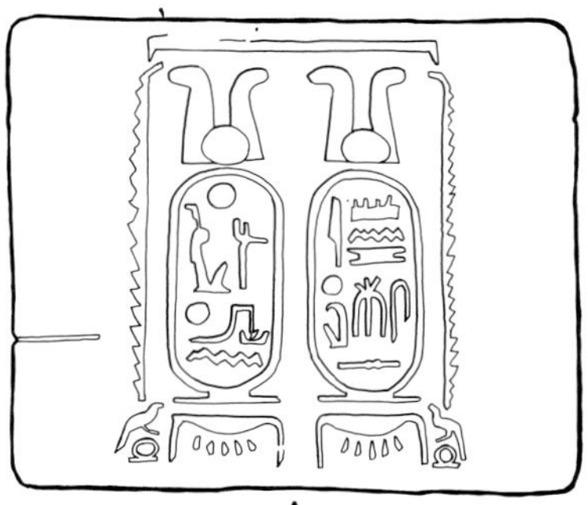

A

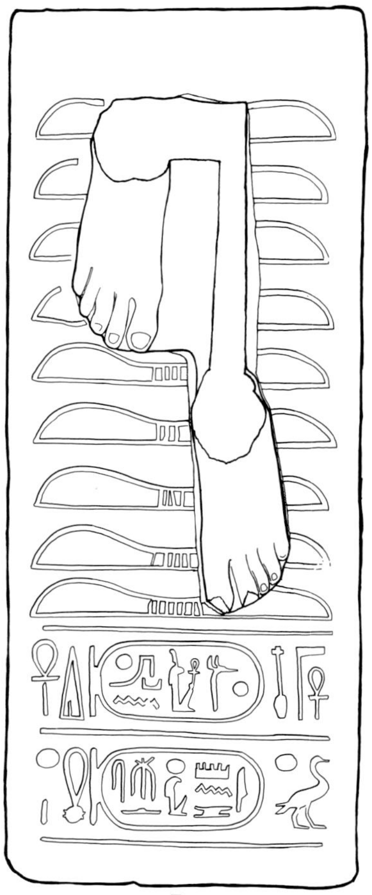

E

B

C

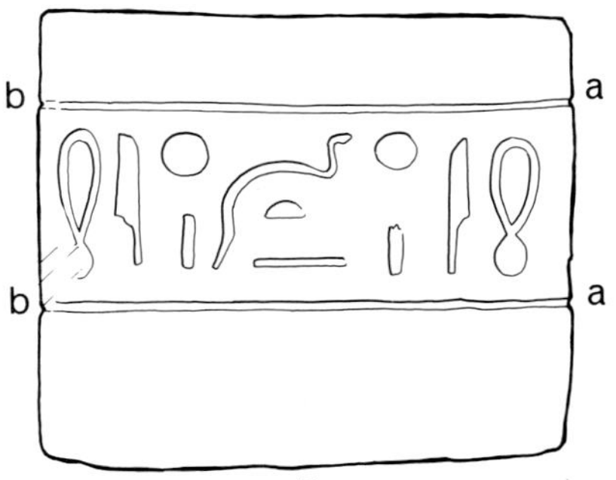

D

0 1 5 CM

29282

Not to scale

Not to scale

1. 1231

2. 68675

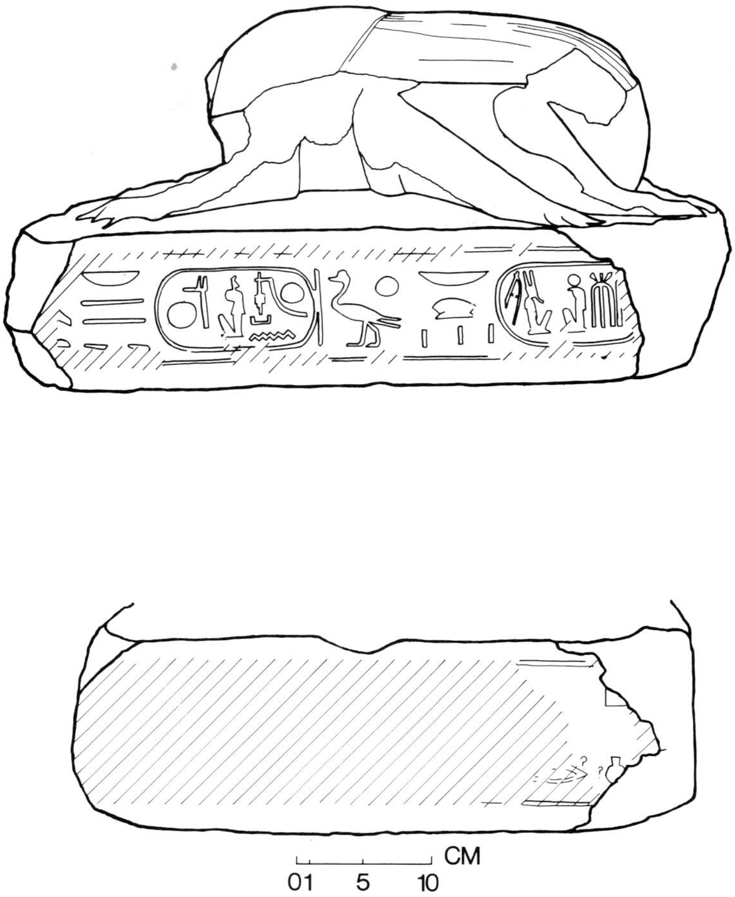

1. 1231

2. 68675

1. 29951

29952

2. 54420

3. 68173

1. 29951

29952

2. 54420

3. 68173

1784

1784

66668

66668

1. 66667

2. 1654

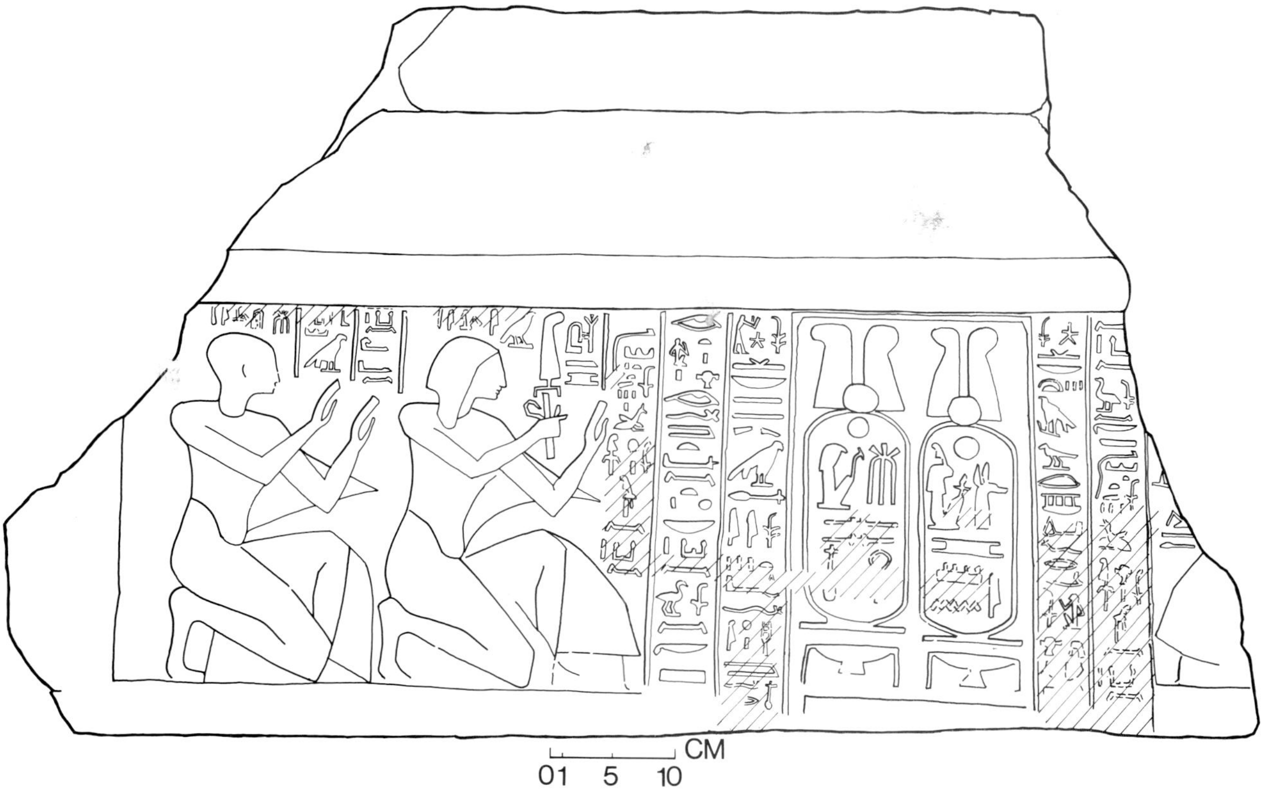

1. 66667

2. 1654

1. 142

2. 107

1. 142

2. 107

1. 1198

2. 1726

1. 1198

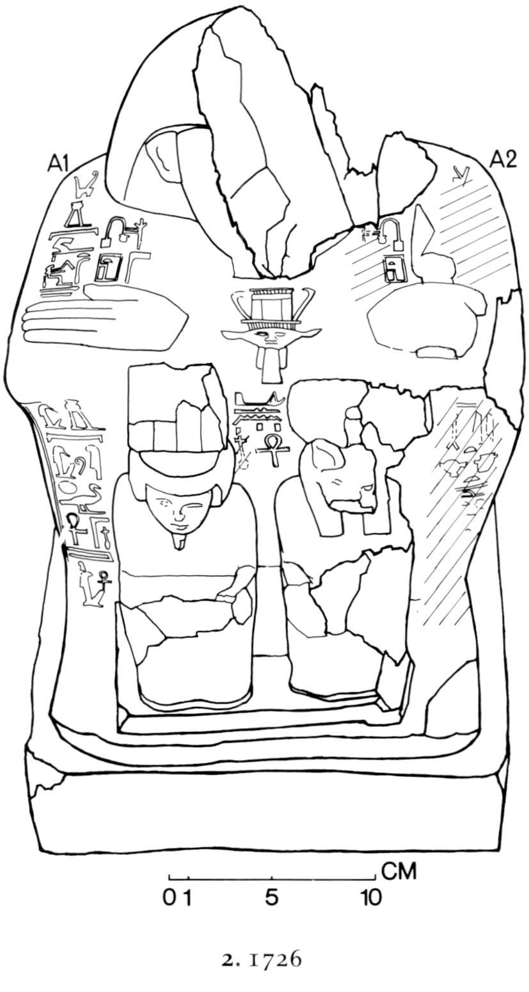

2. 1726

1726

B
CM
0 1 5 10

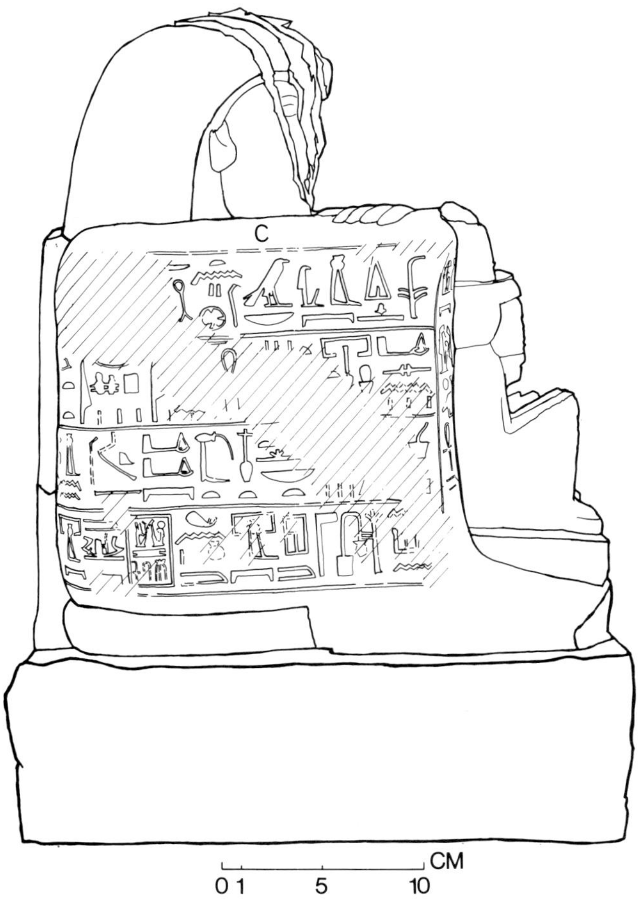
C
CM
0 1 5 10

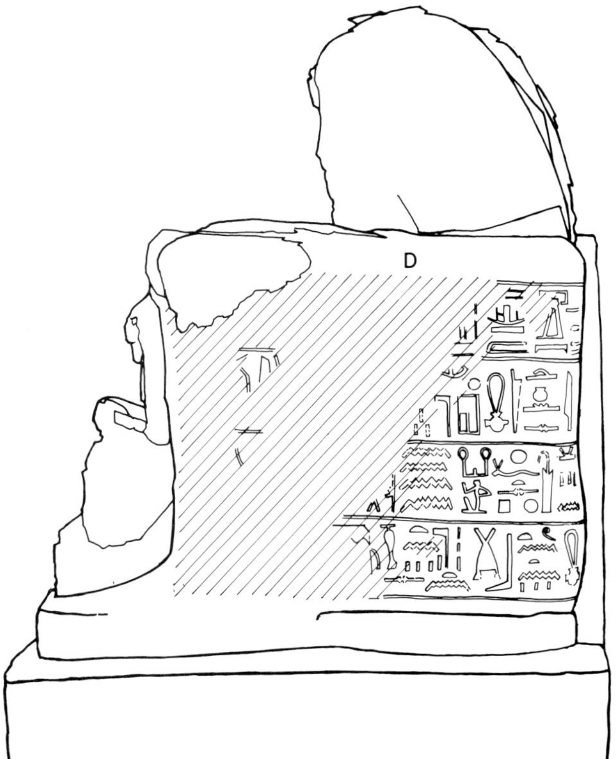
D
CM
0 1 5 10

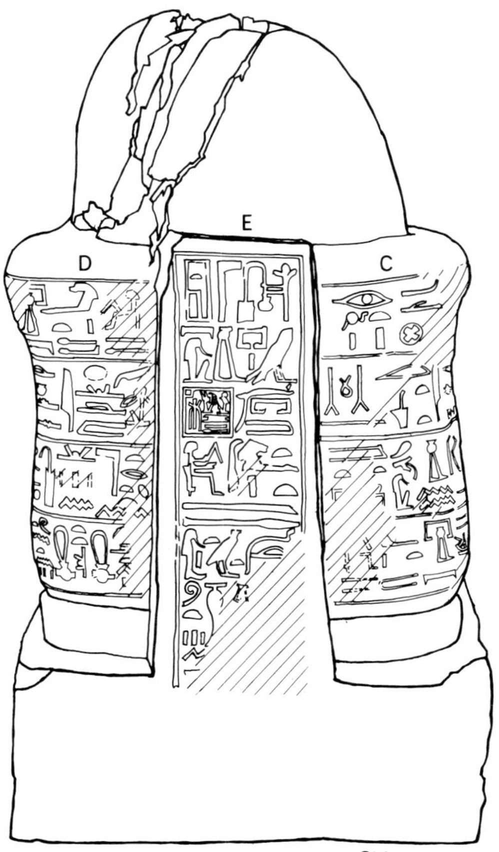
E
D
C
CM
0 1 5 10

1. 65593

2. 2559

1. 65593

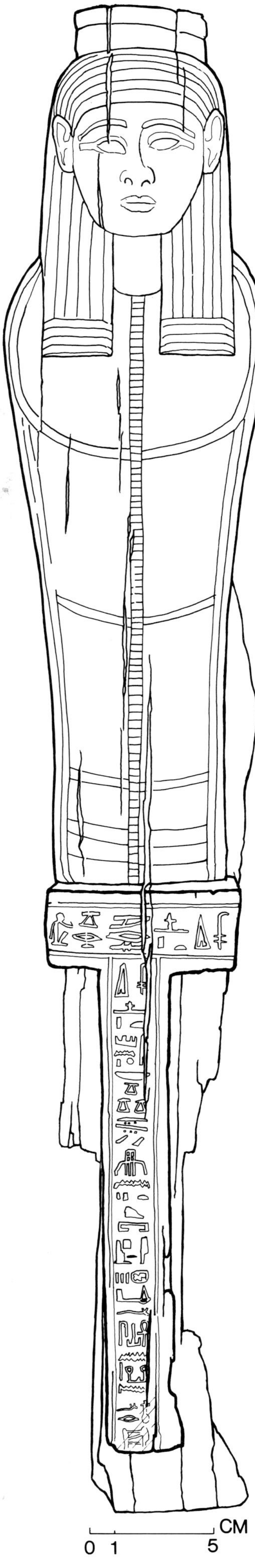

2. 2559

2. 555

1. 269

2. 555

1. 269

2. 341

1. 264

1. 264

2. 341

2. 816

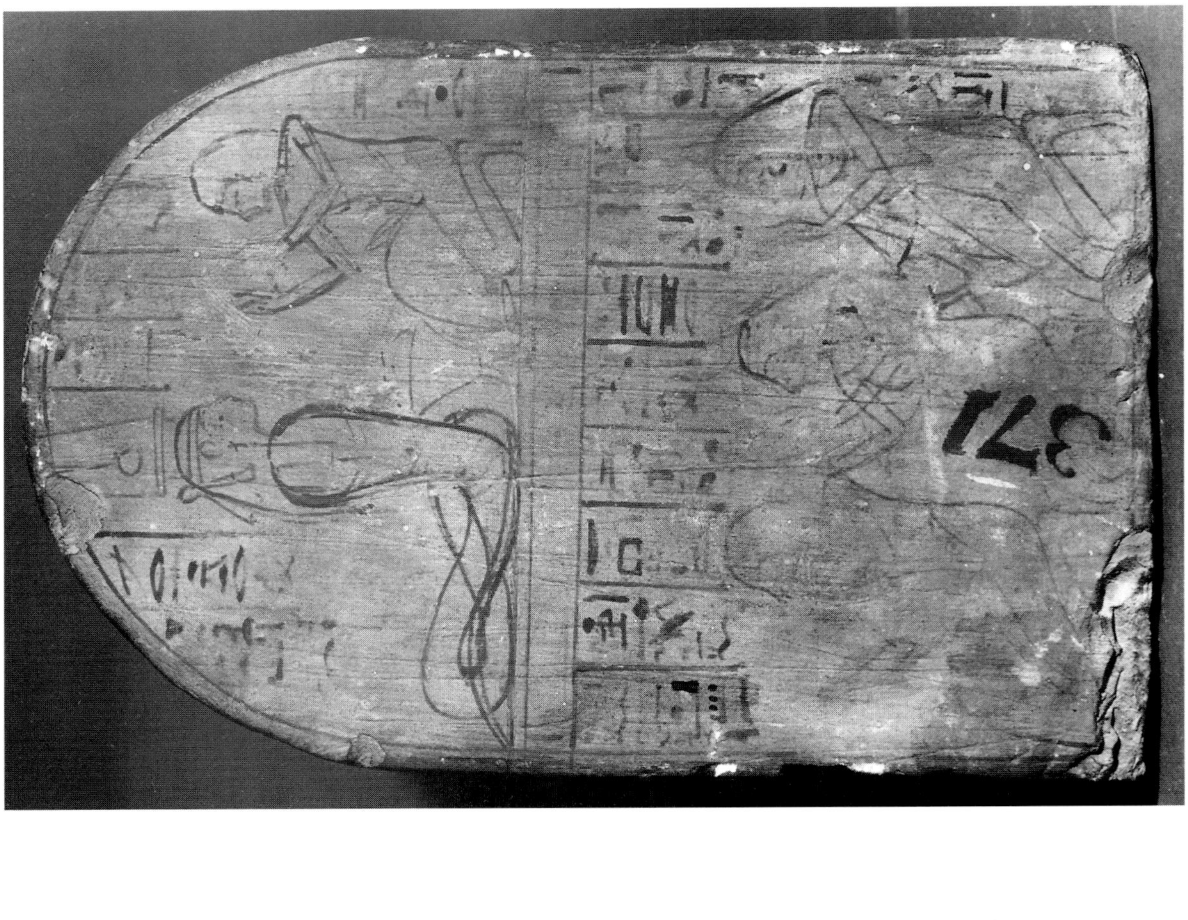

1. 371

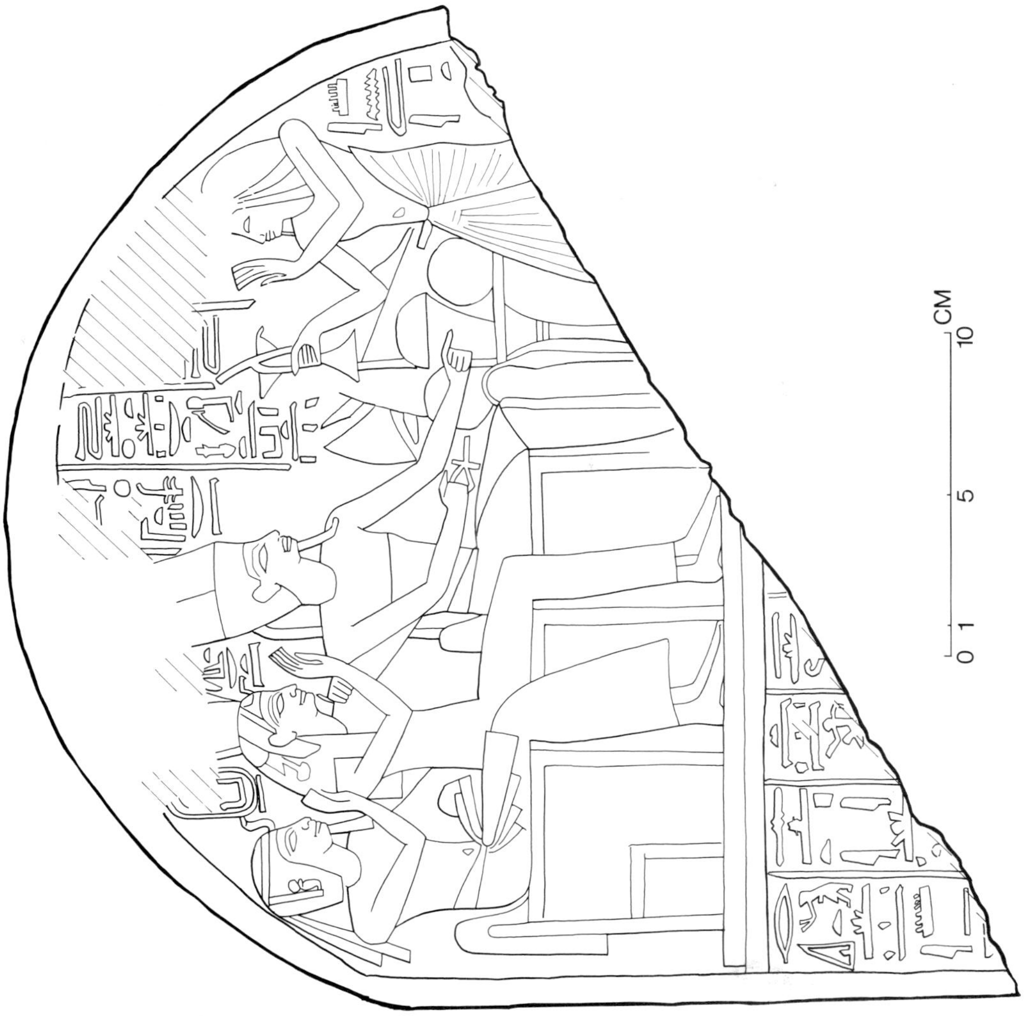

2.816

1.371

2. 814

1. 284

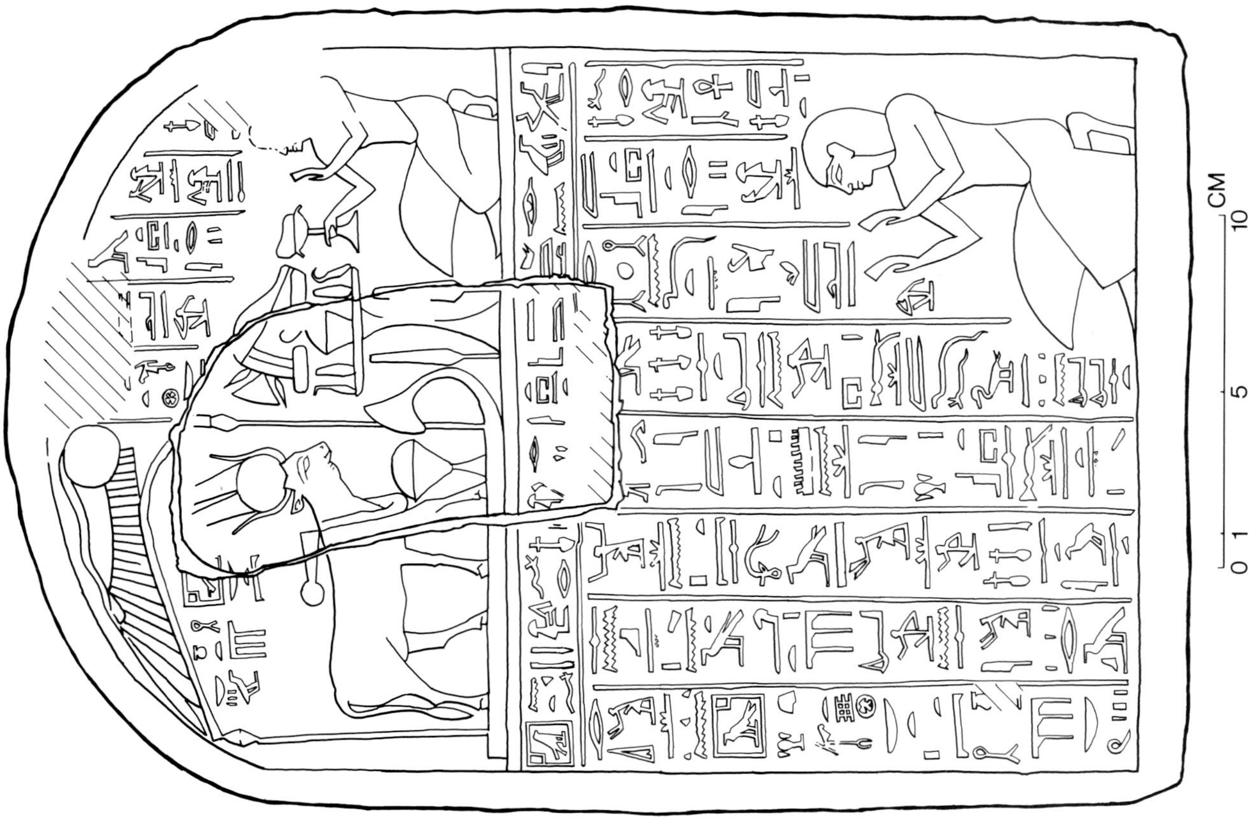

2. 814

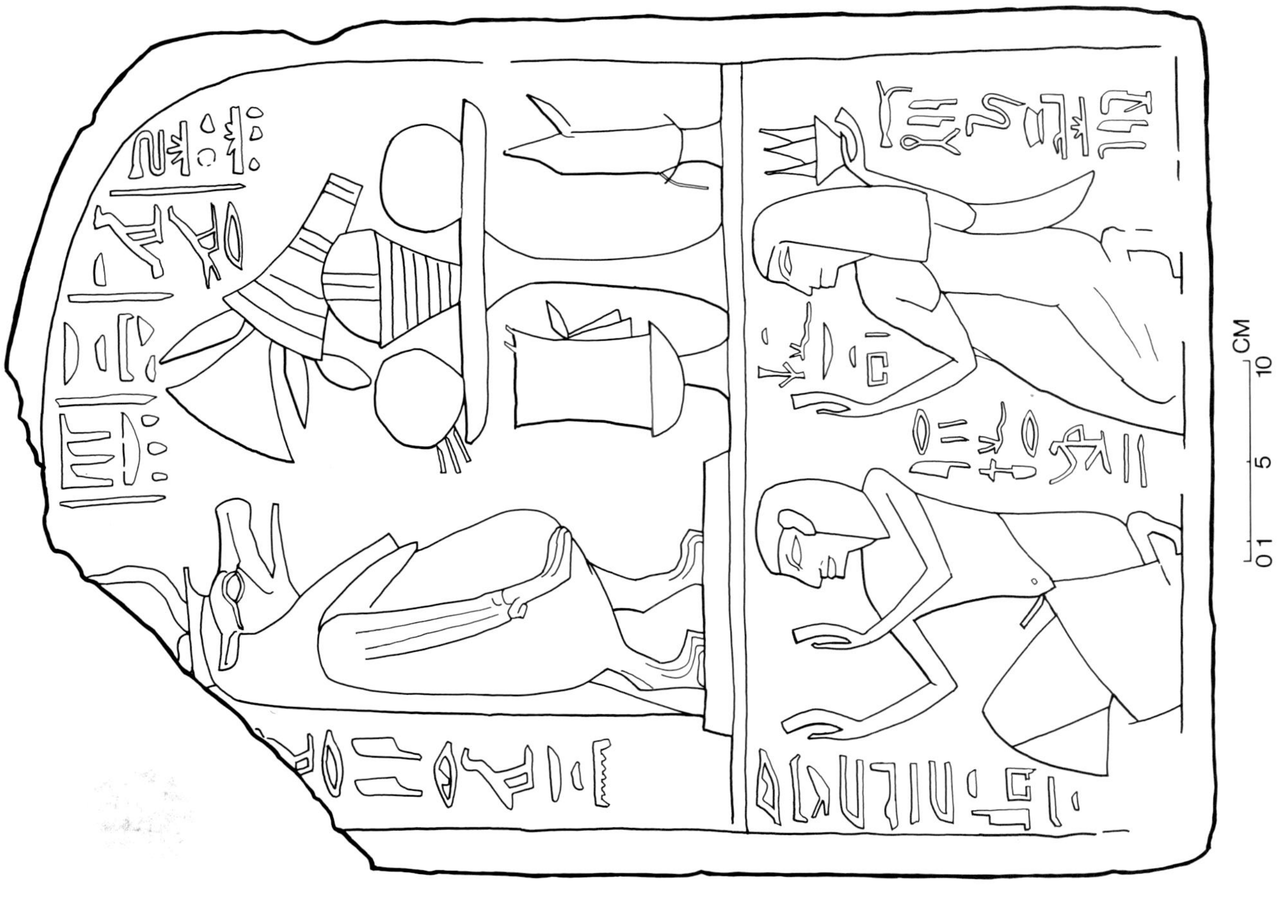

1. 284

2. 271

1. 1347

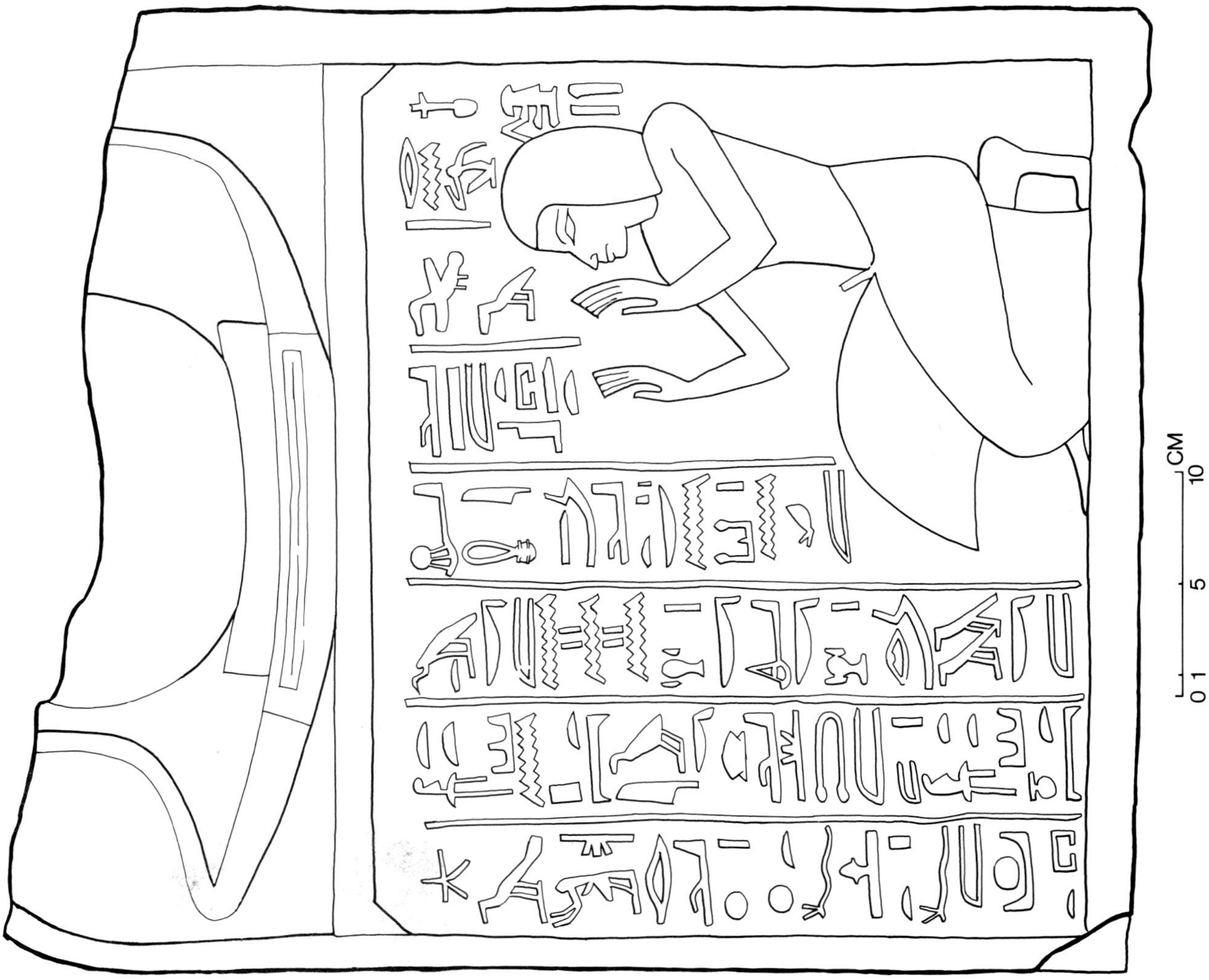

2. 271

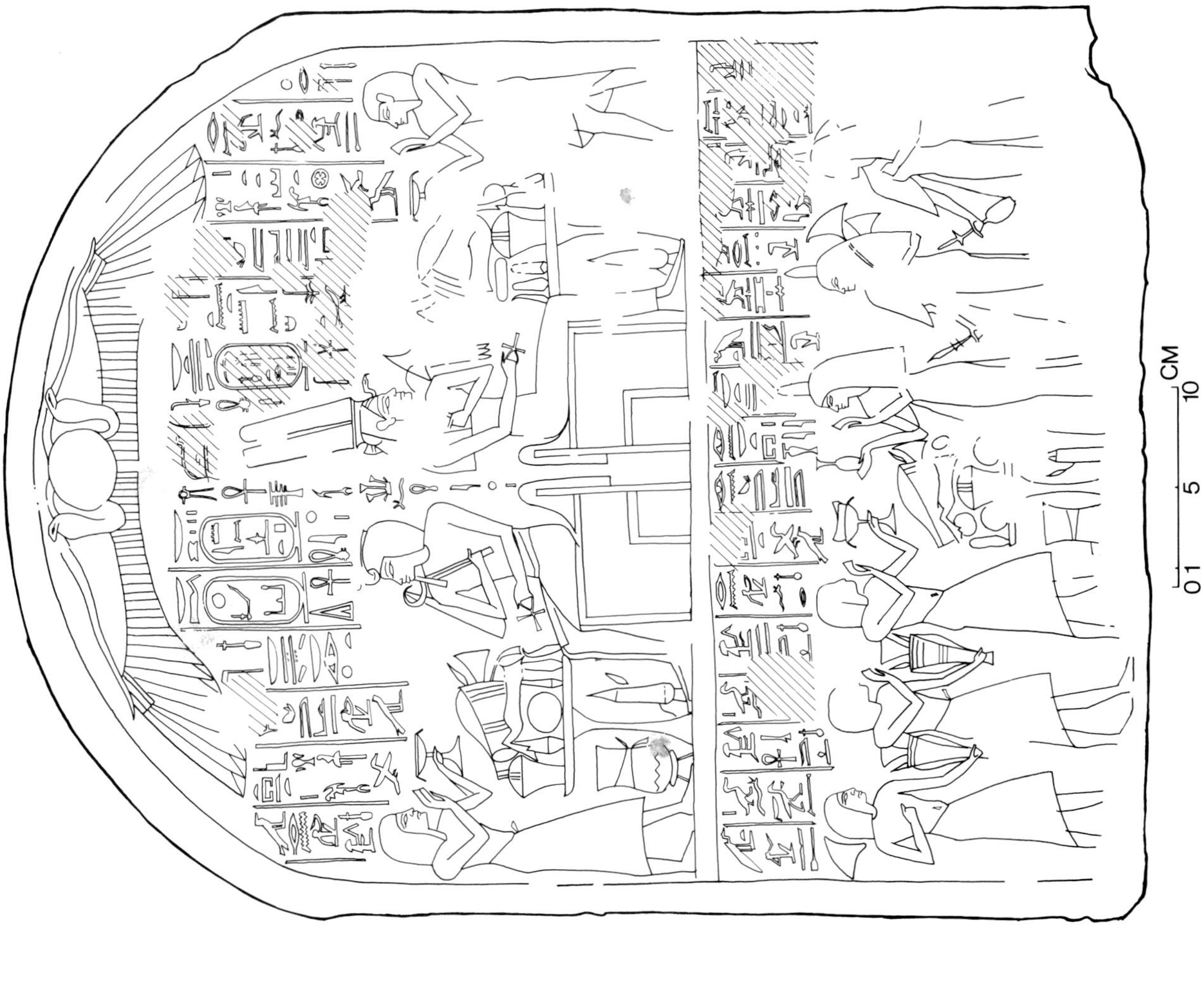

1. 1347

1. 286

2. 446

1. 286

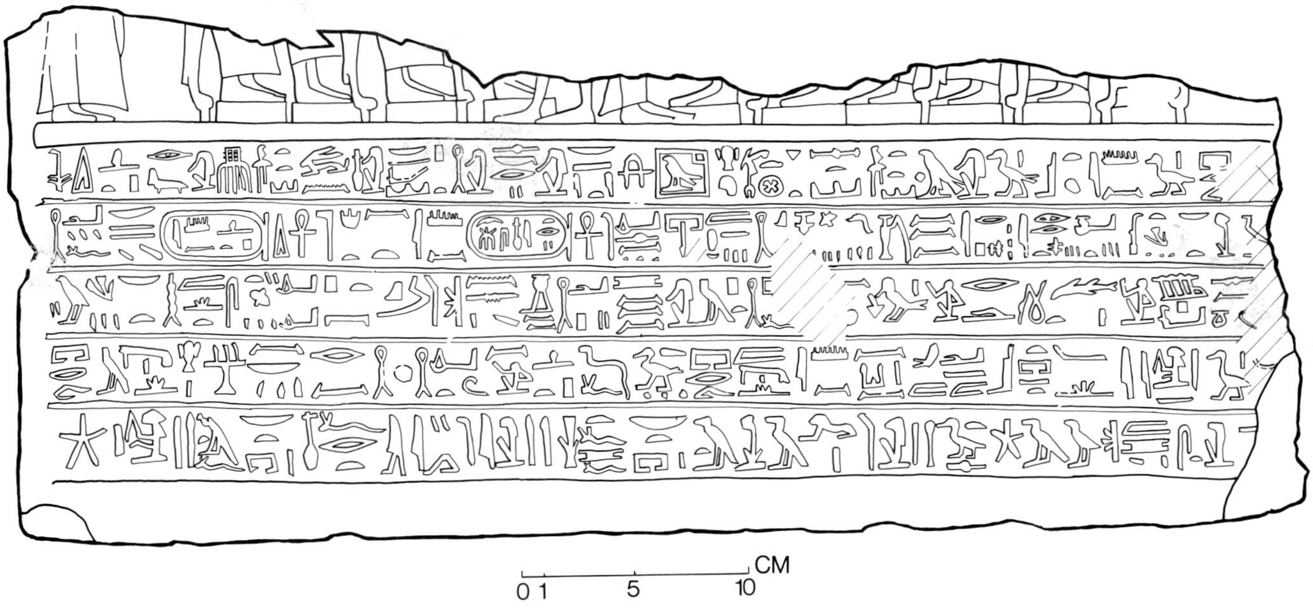

2. 446

63783

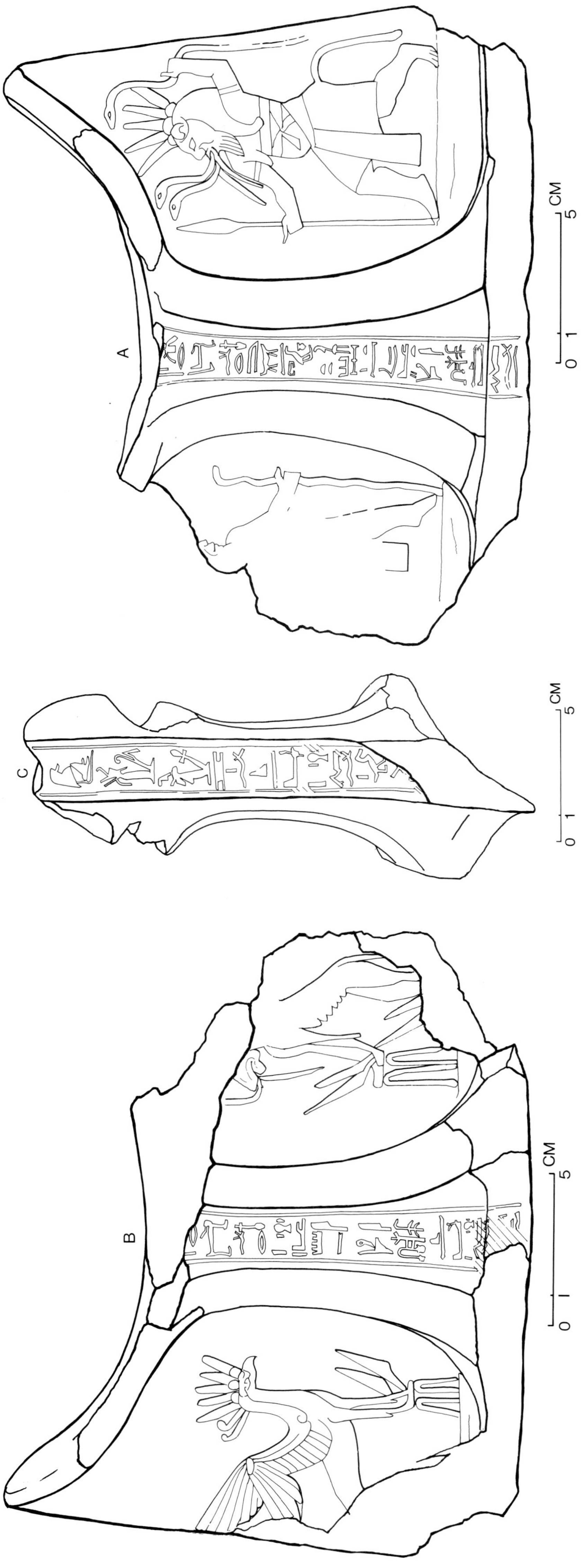

63783

1. 69089

2. 547

1. 69089

2. 547

2. 332

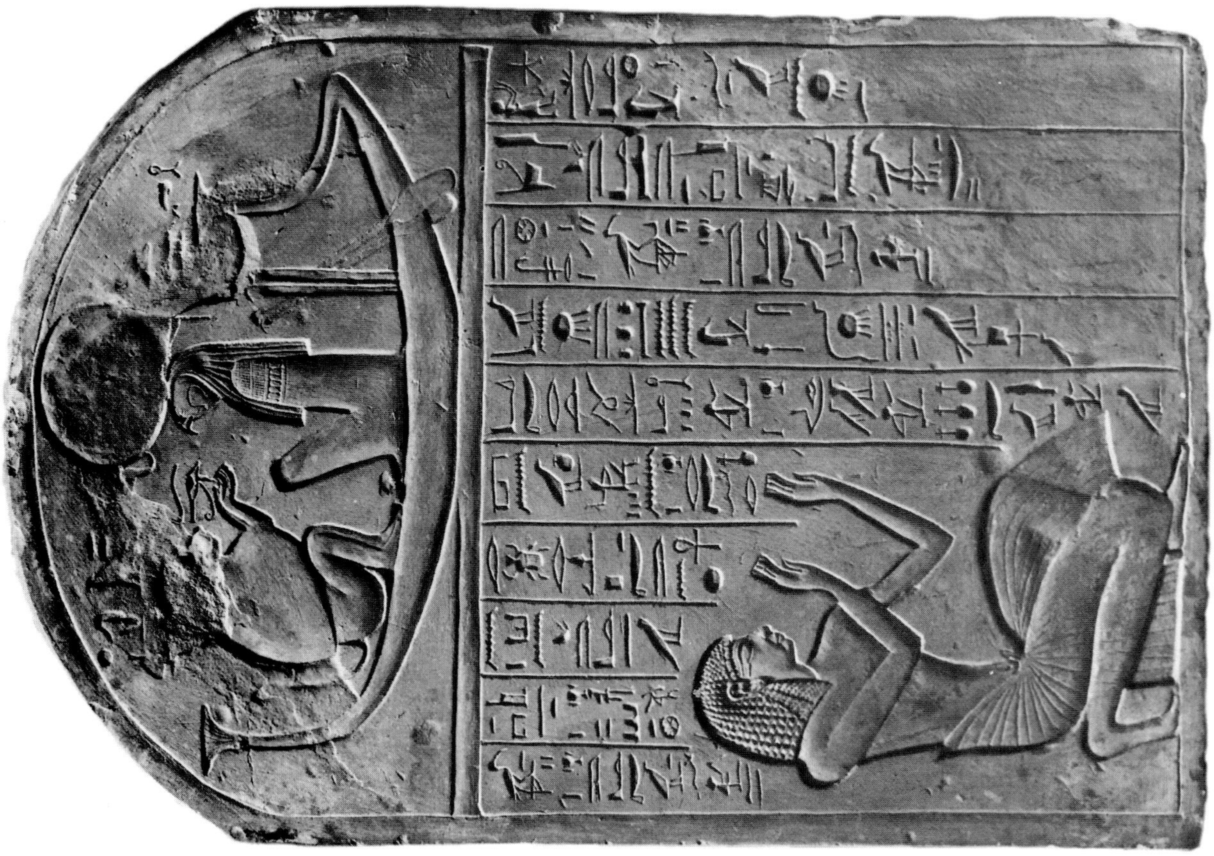

1. 266

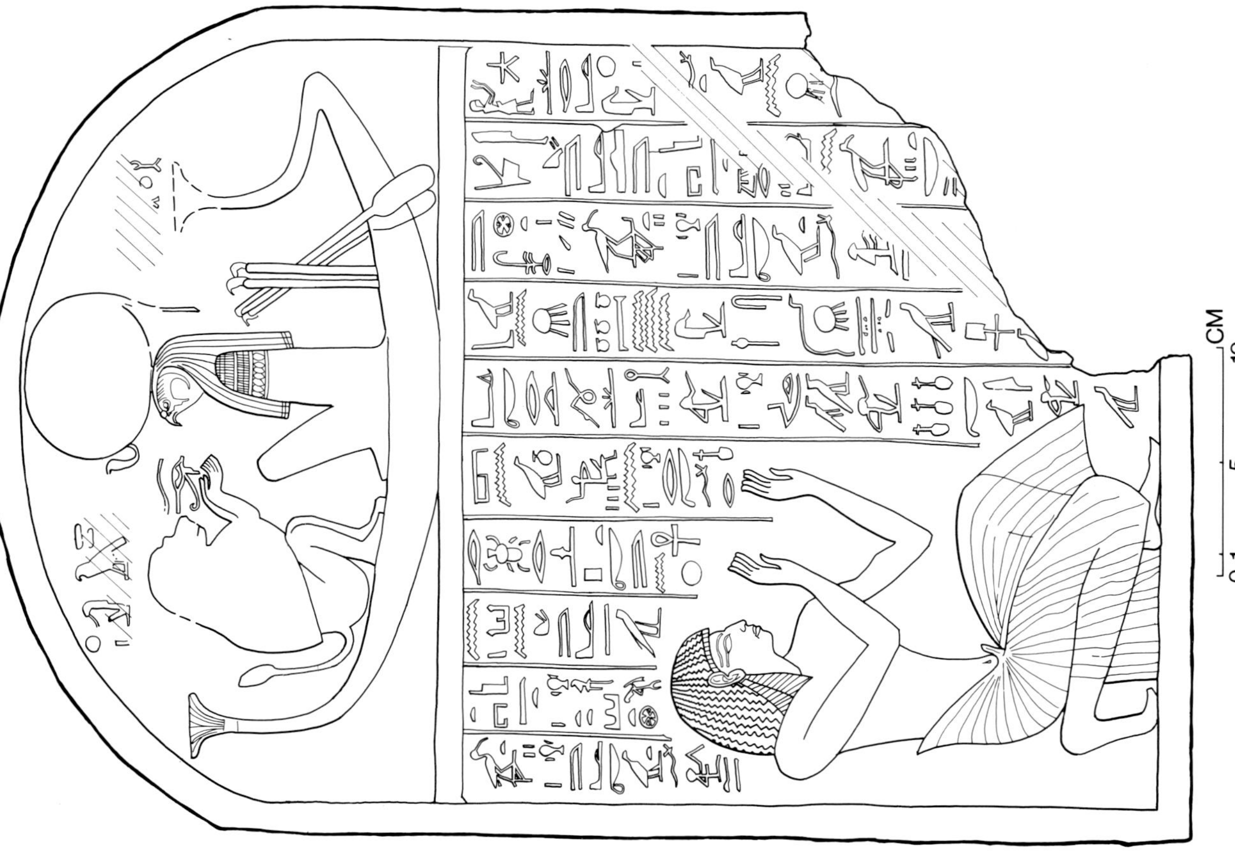

1. 266

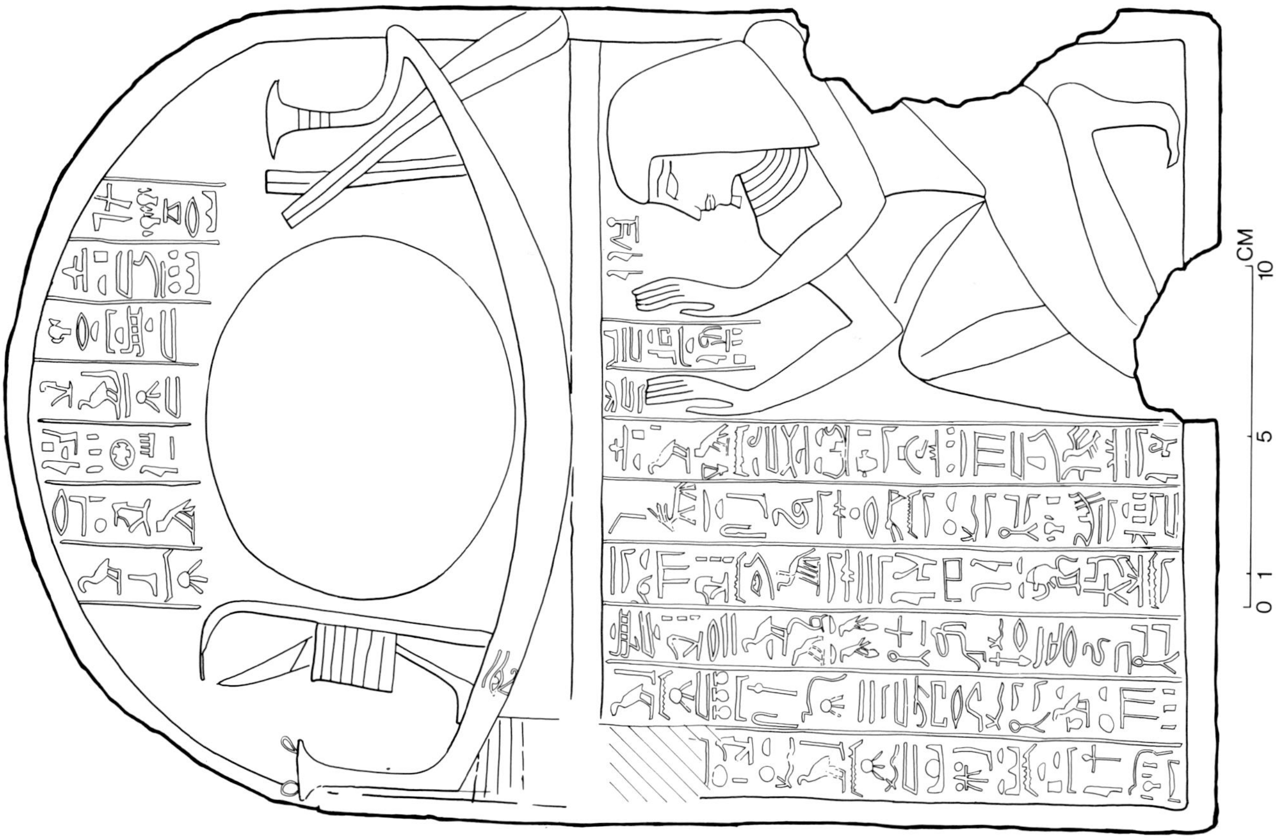

2. 332

Not to s

12247

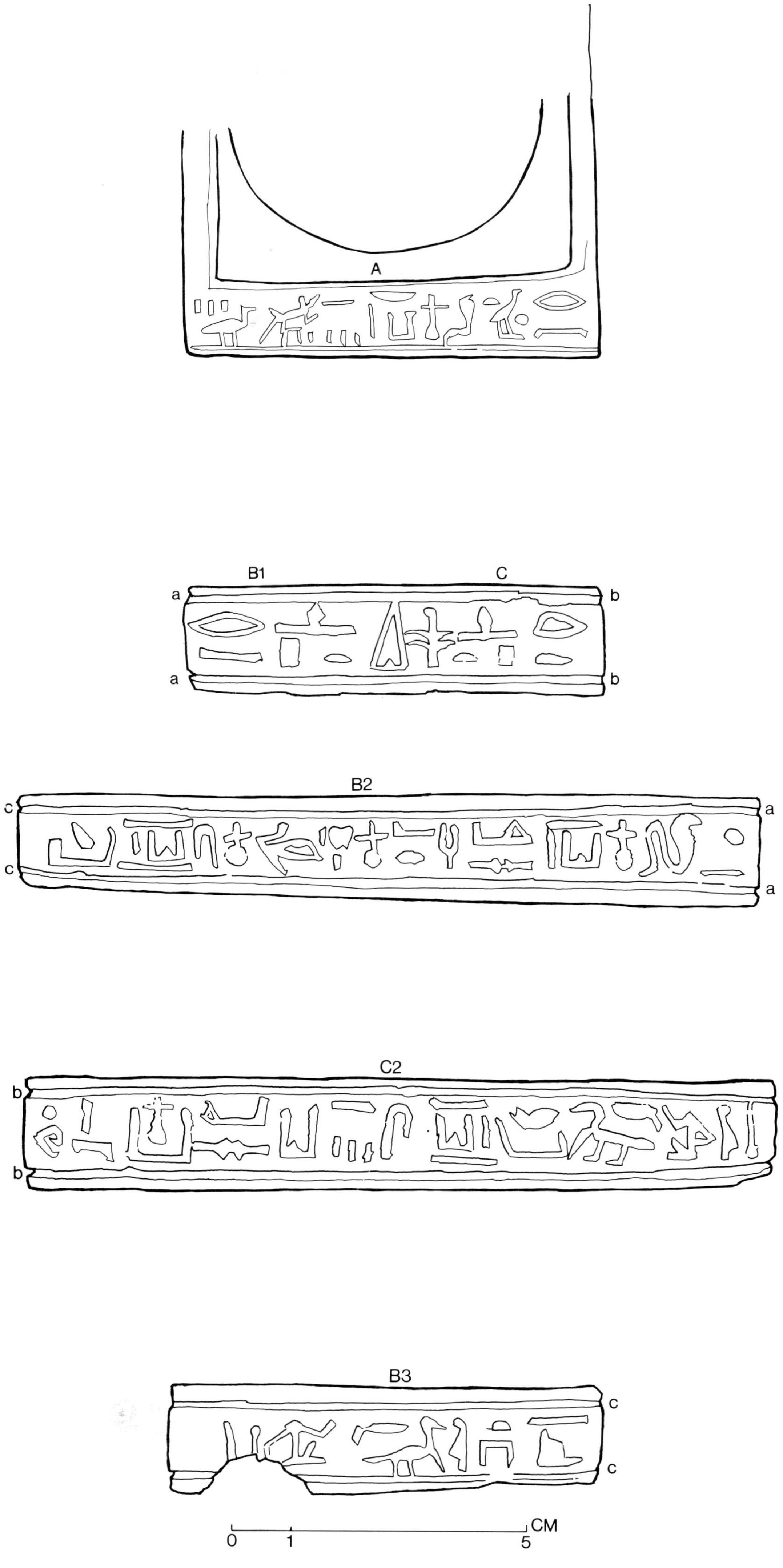
A
B1
C
a
b
B2
c
C2
B3
CM
0
1
5

2. 279

1. 374

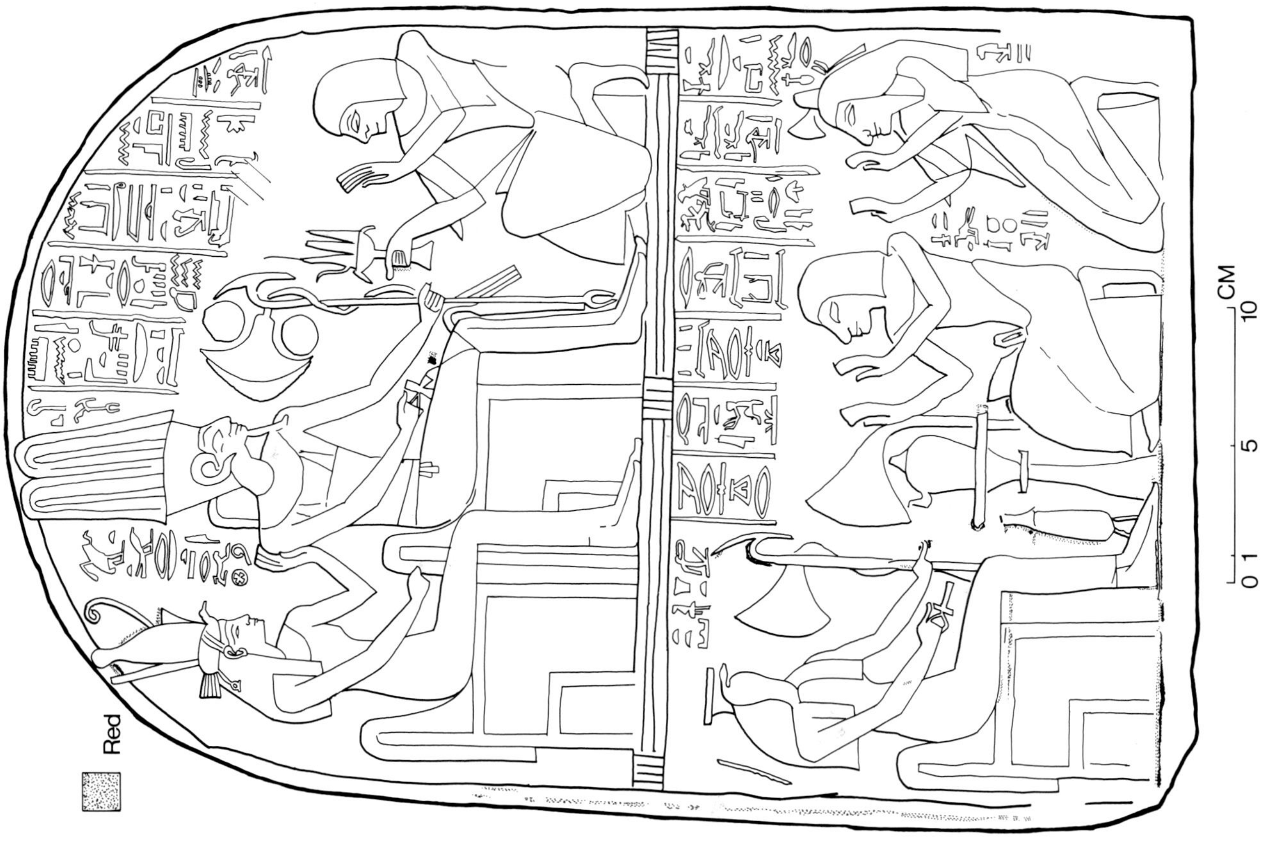

2. 279

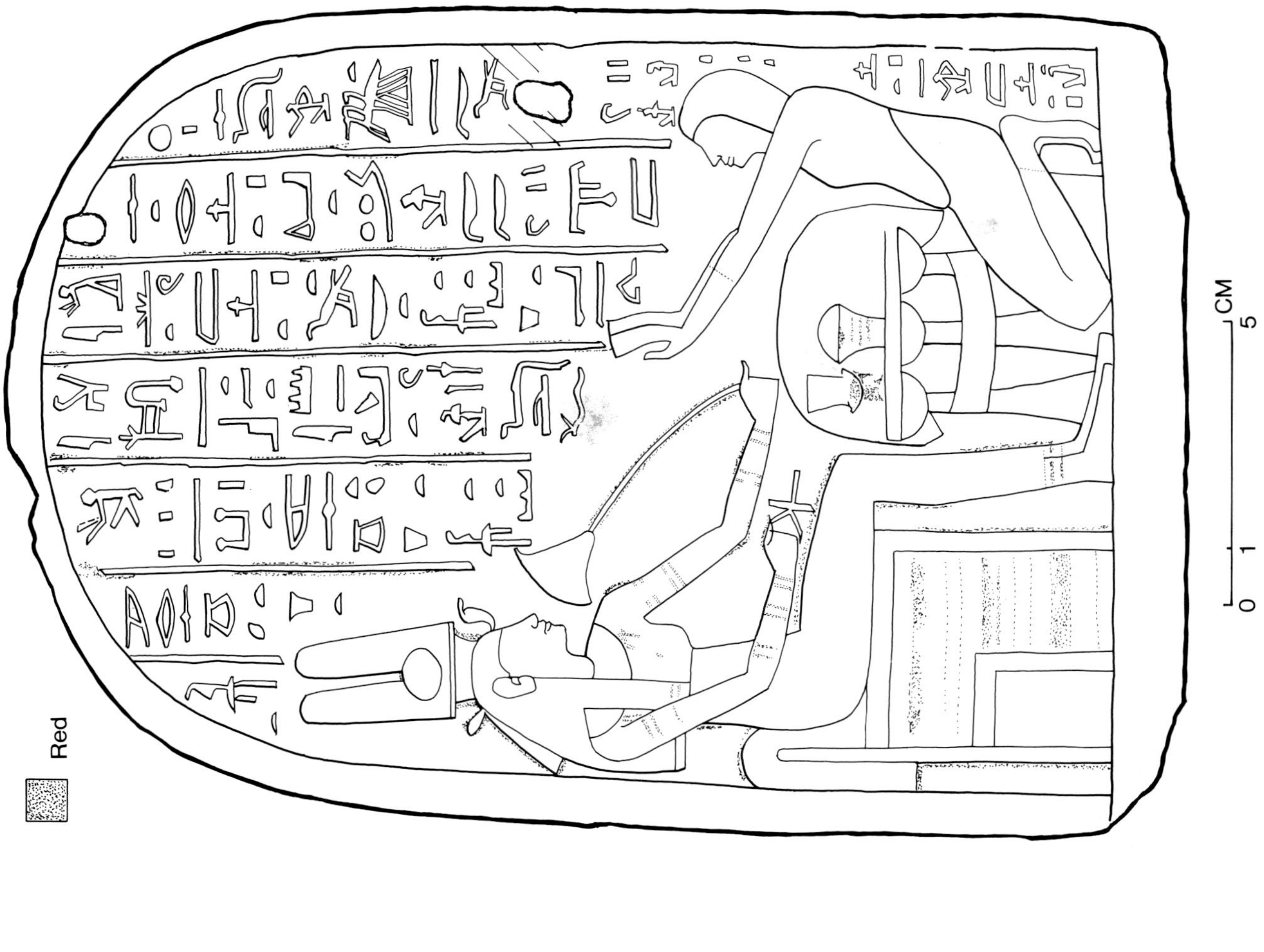

1. 374

2. 812

1. 811

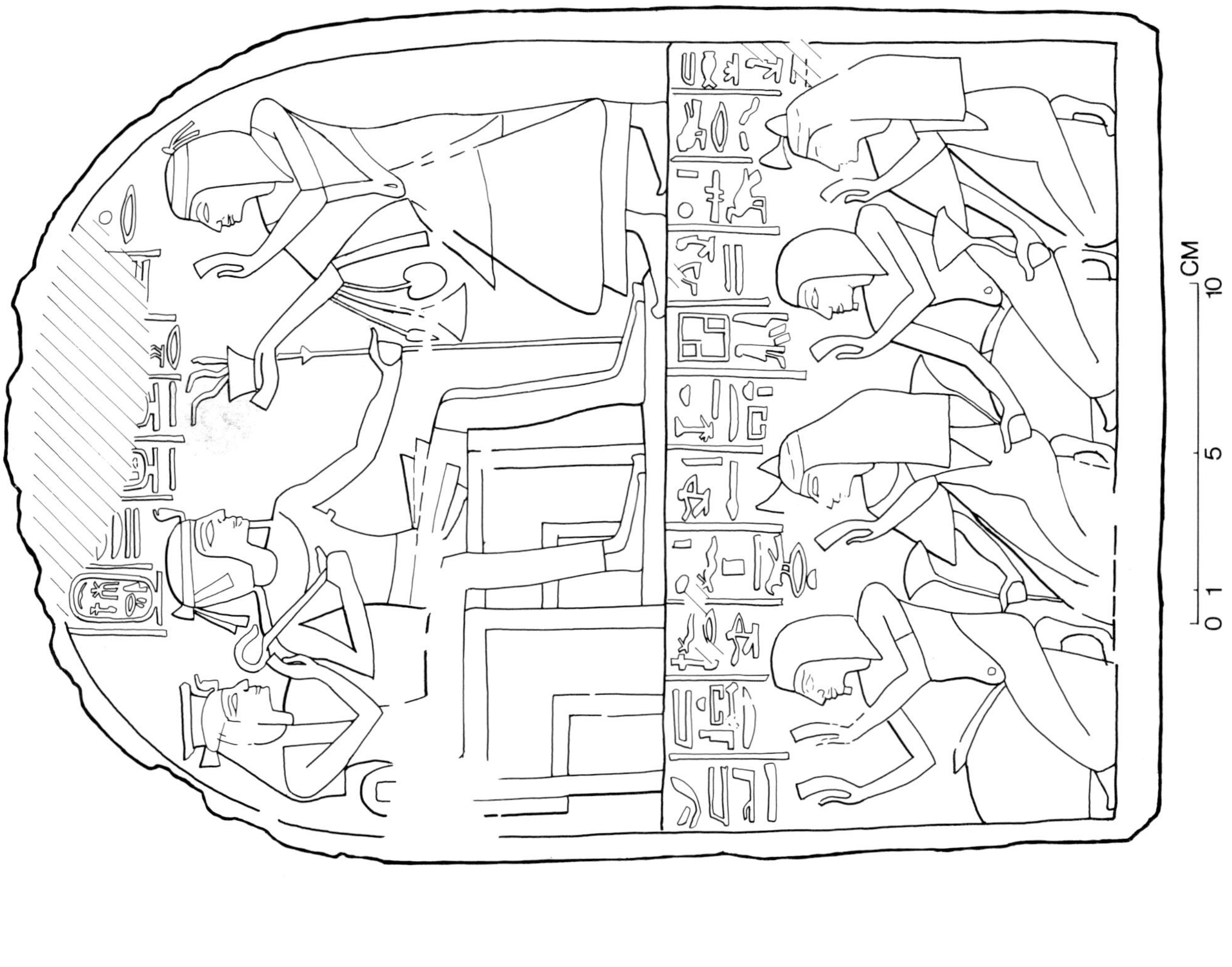

1. 811

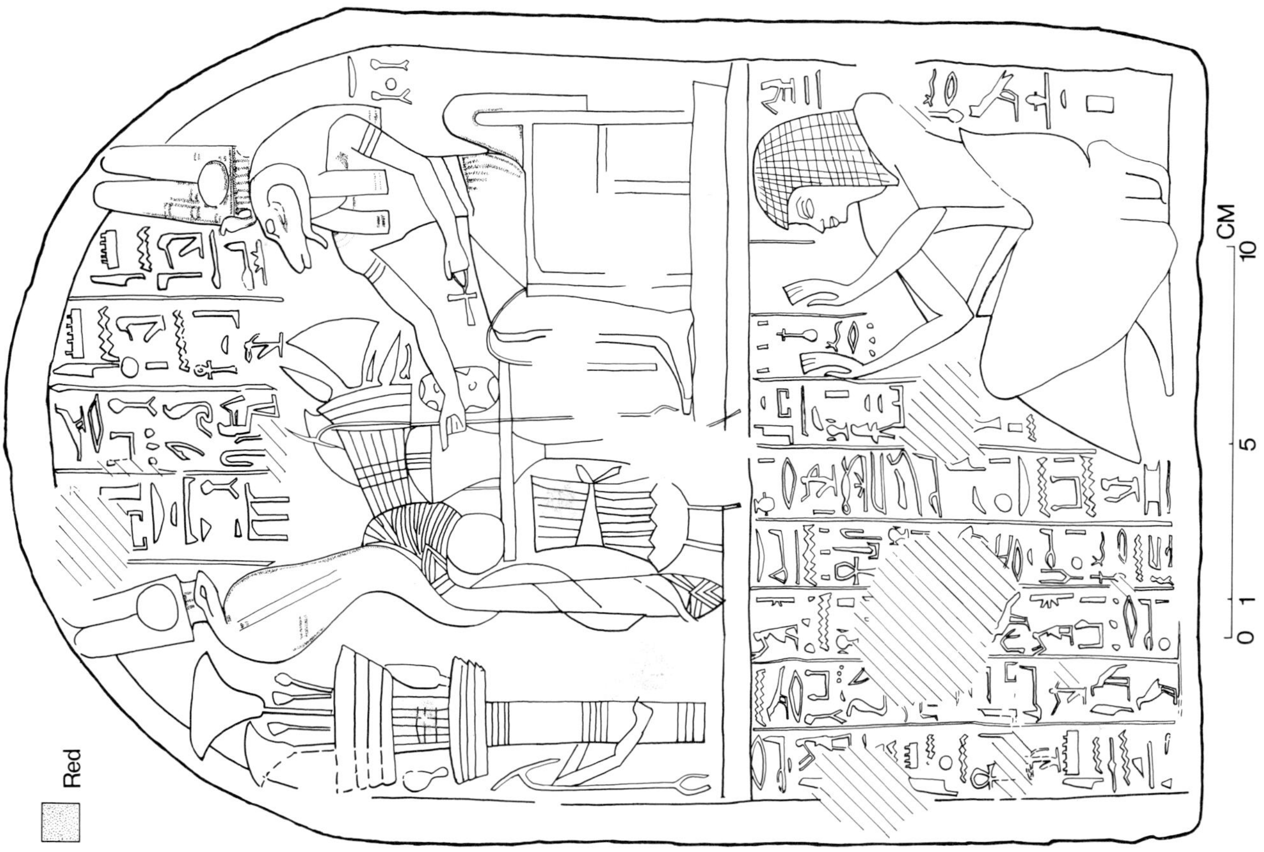

2. 812

2. 277

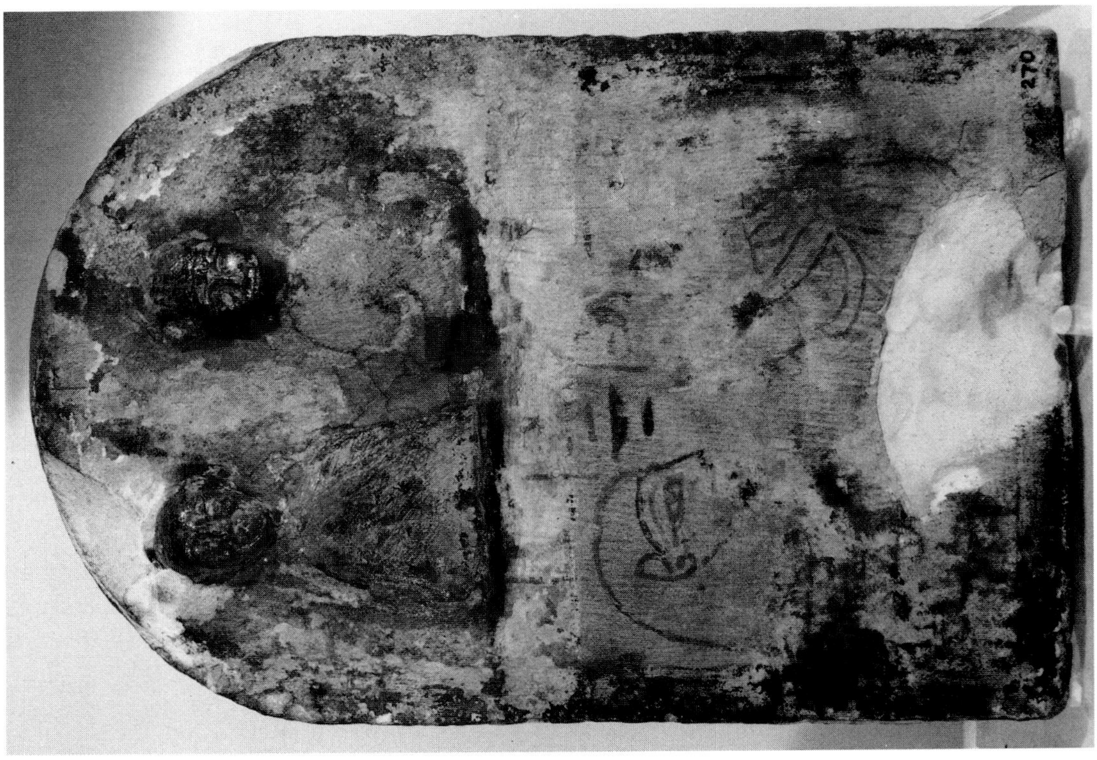

1. 270

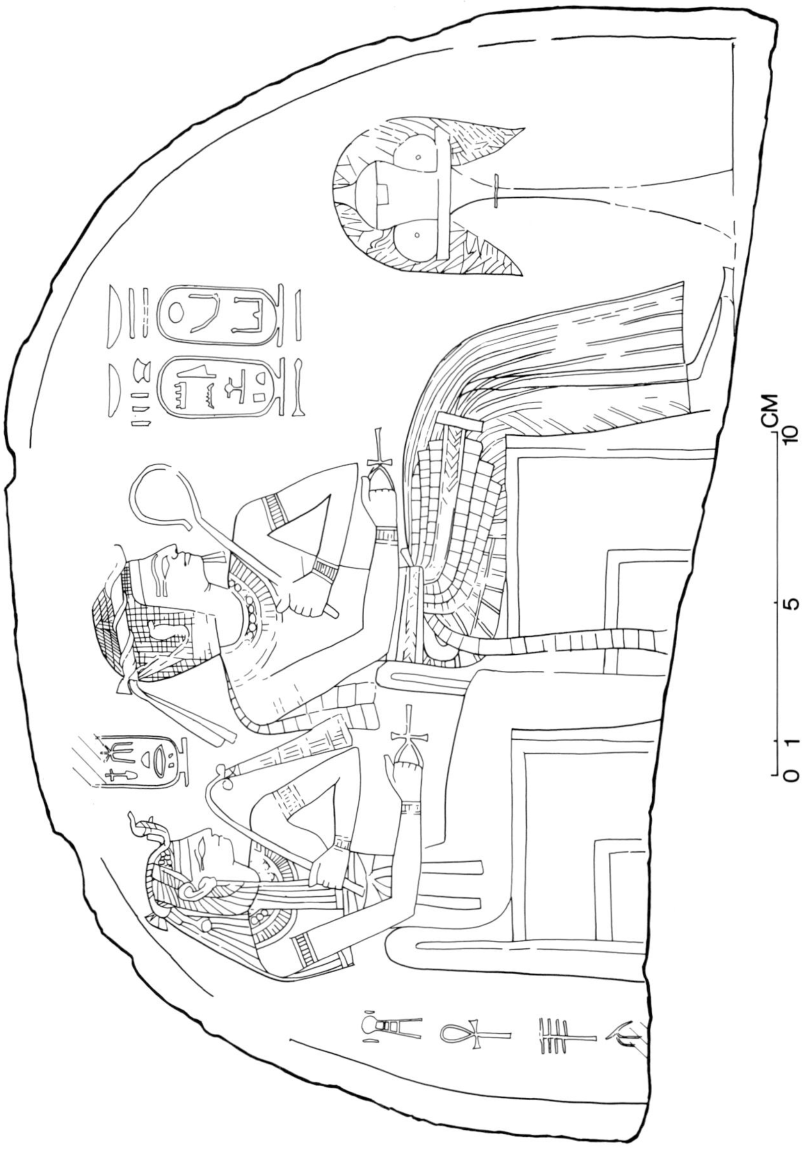

2. 277

1. 270

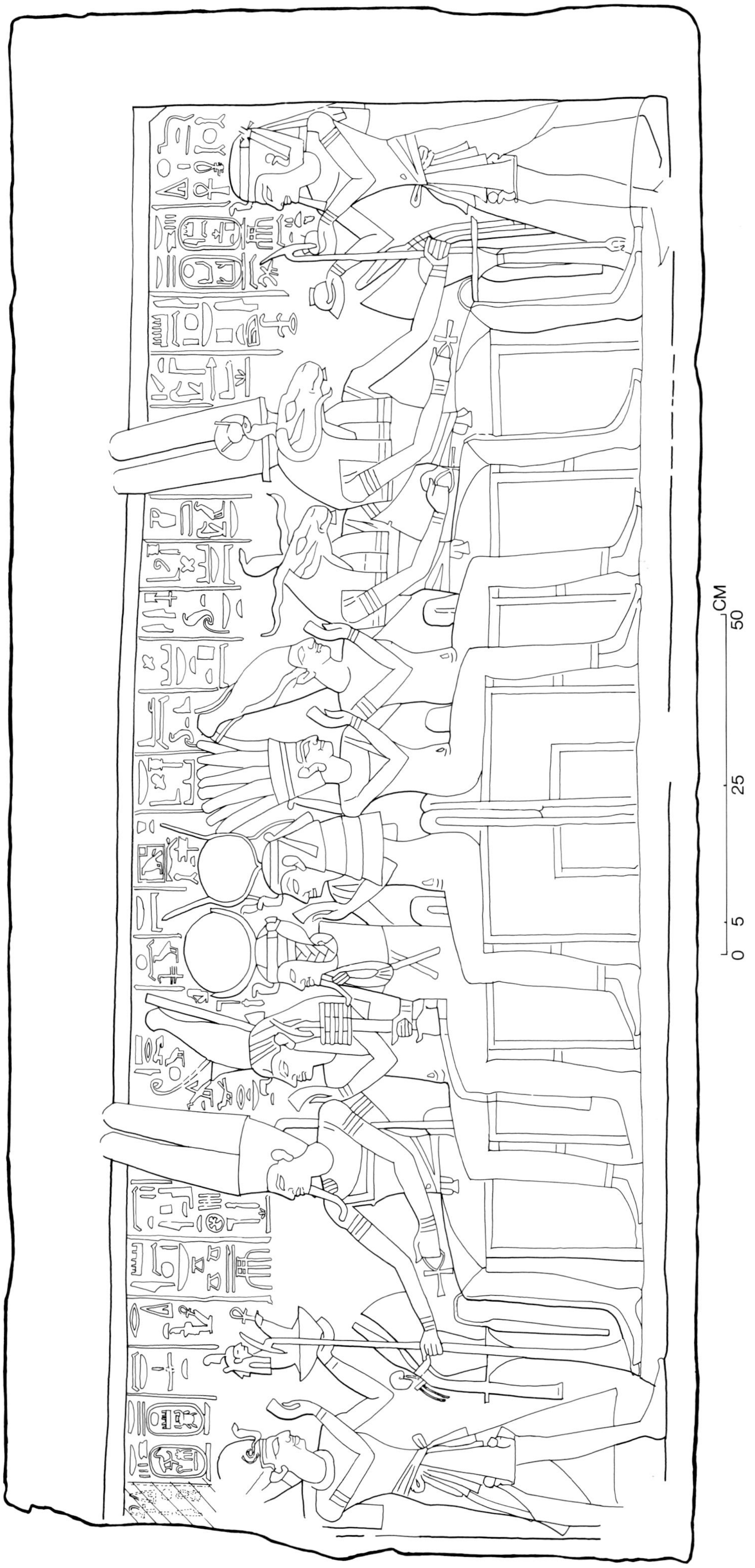
CM
50
25
5
0

2. 292

1. 288

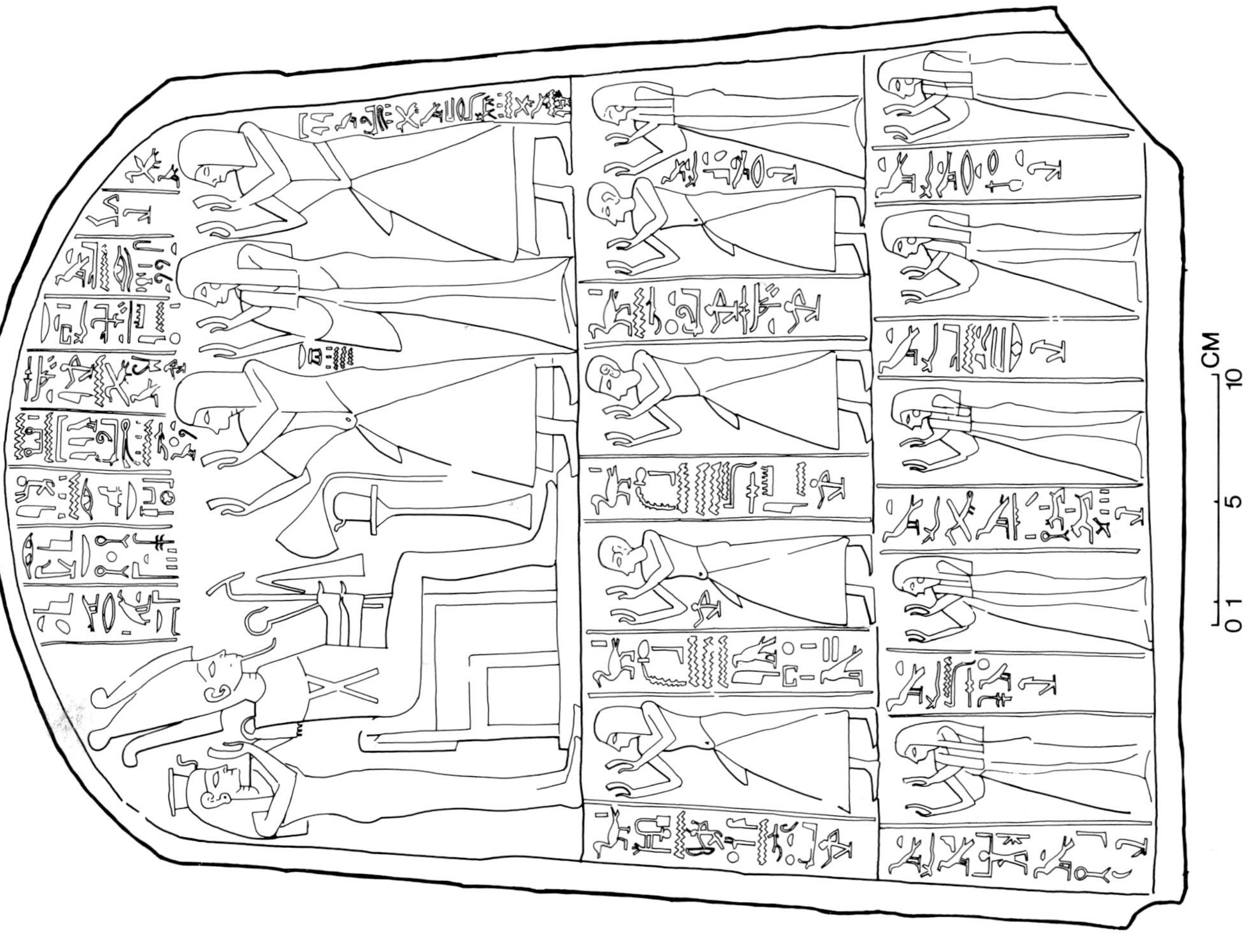

2. 292

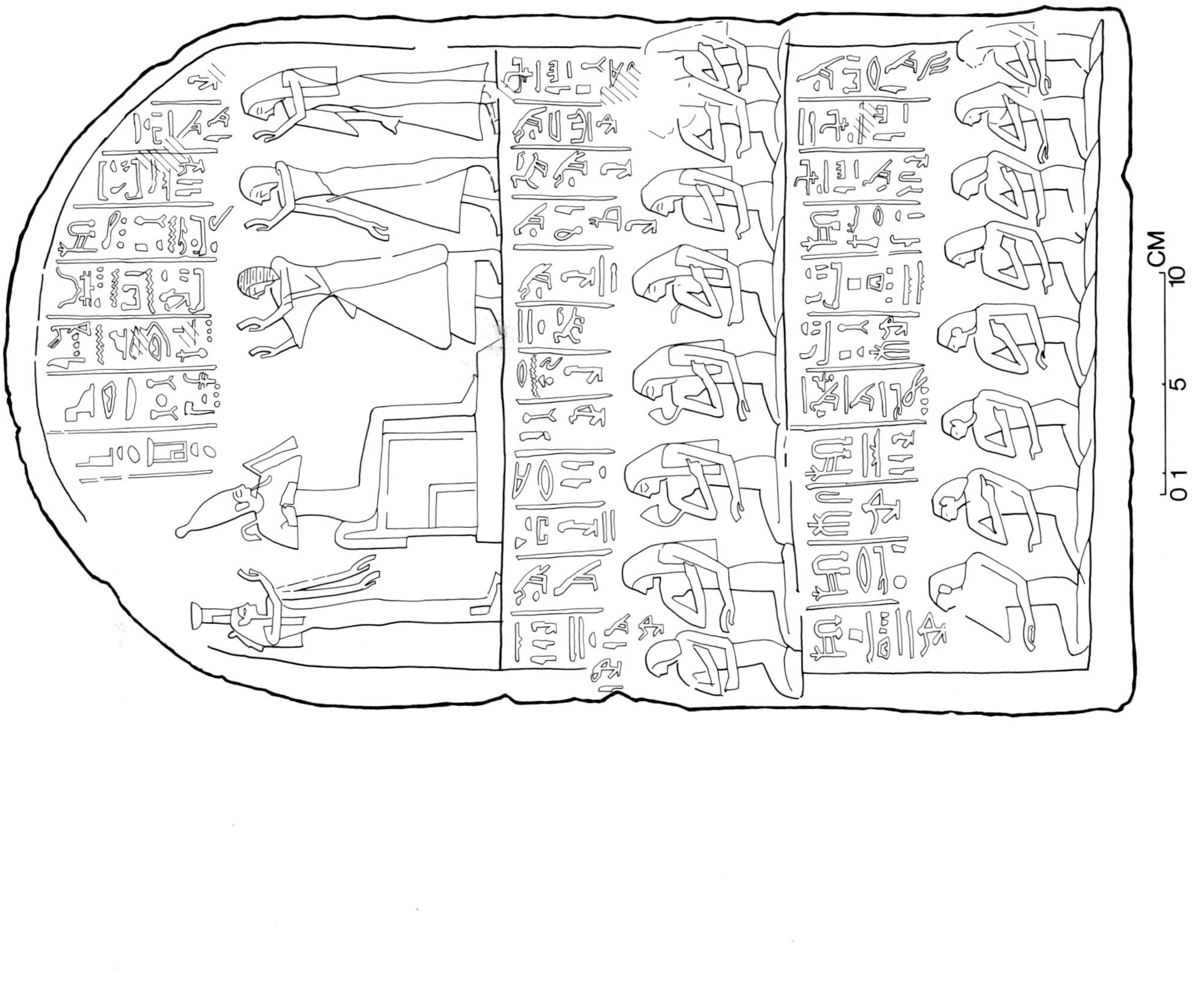

I. 288

2. 349

1. 309

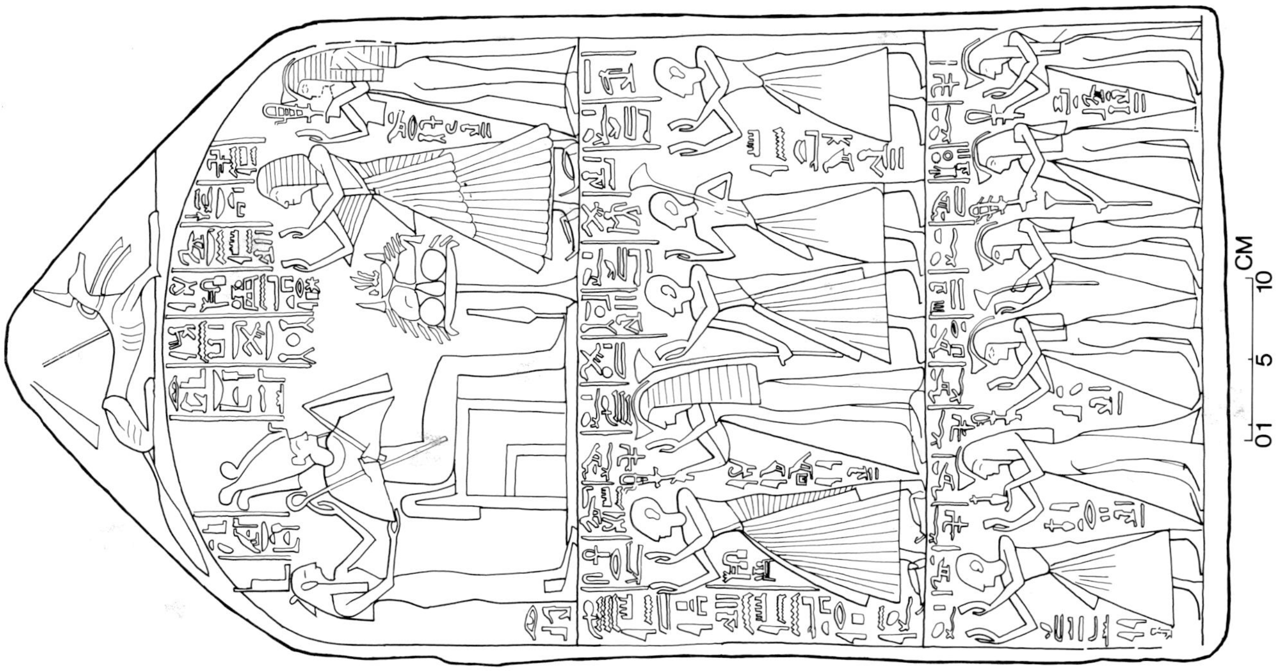

2. 349

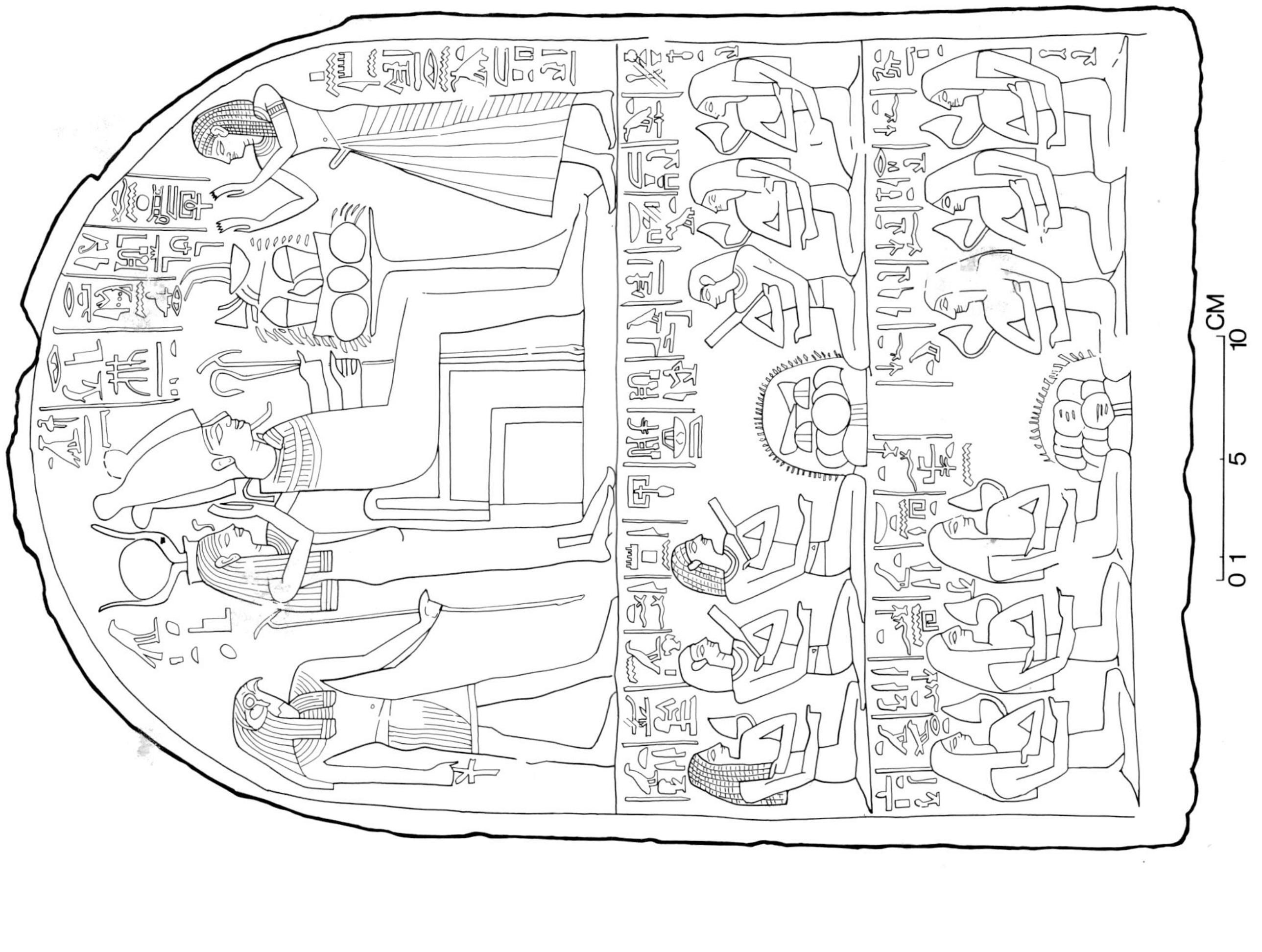

1. 309

549

CM
0 1
5
10

350

B

A

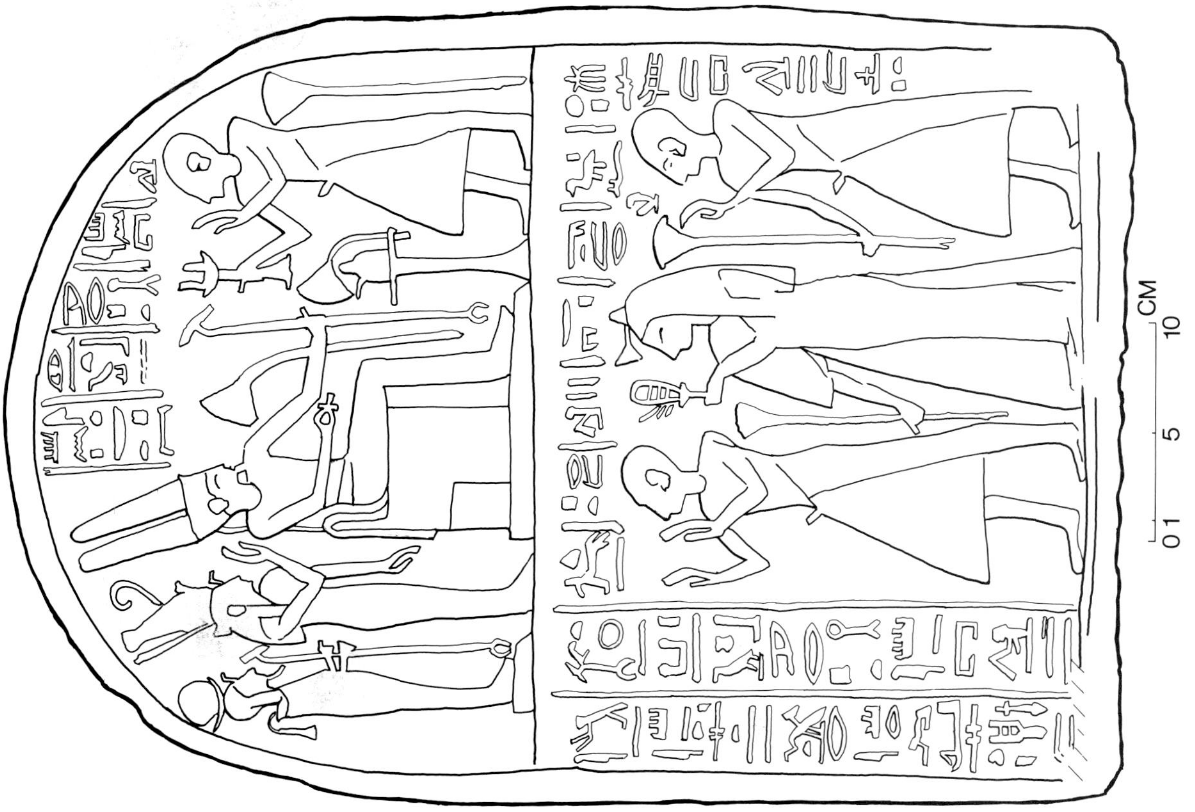

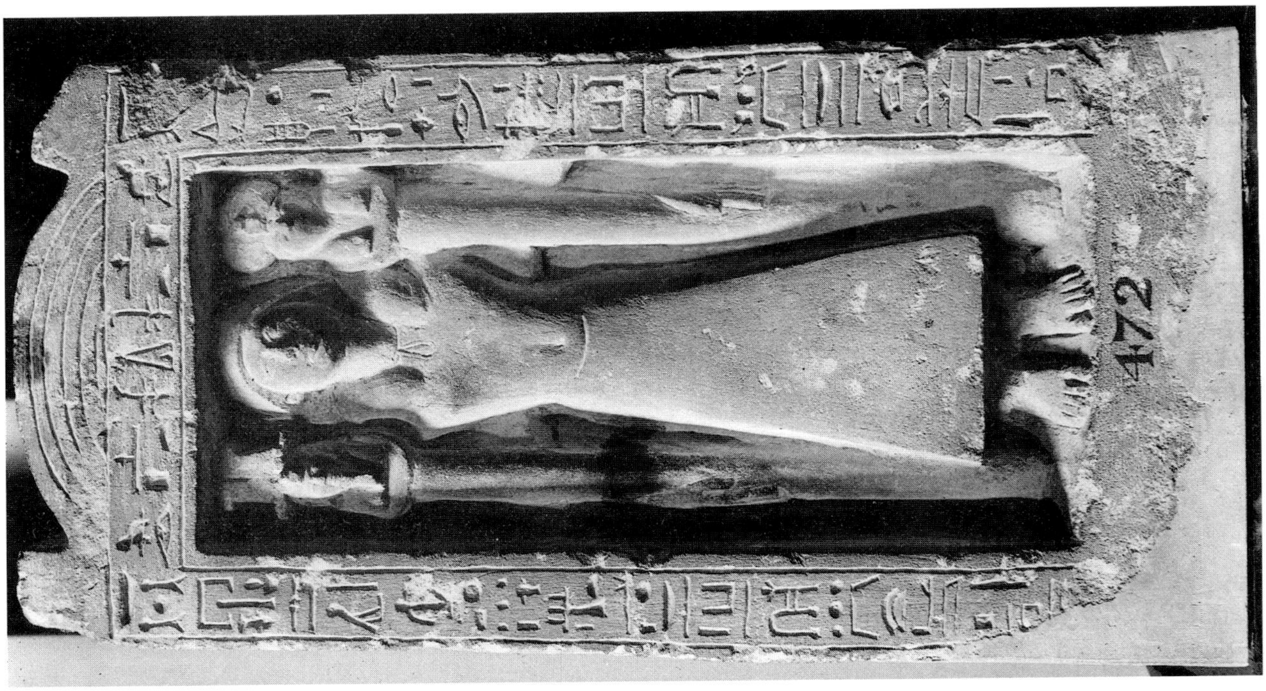

2. 472

1. 351

2.472

1.351

1. 455

2. 646

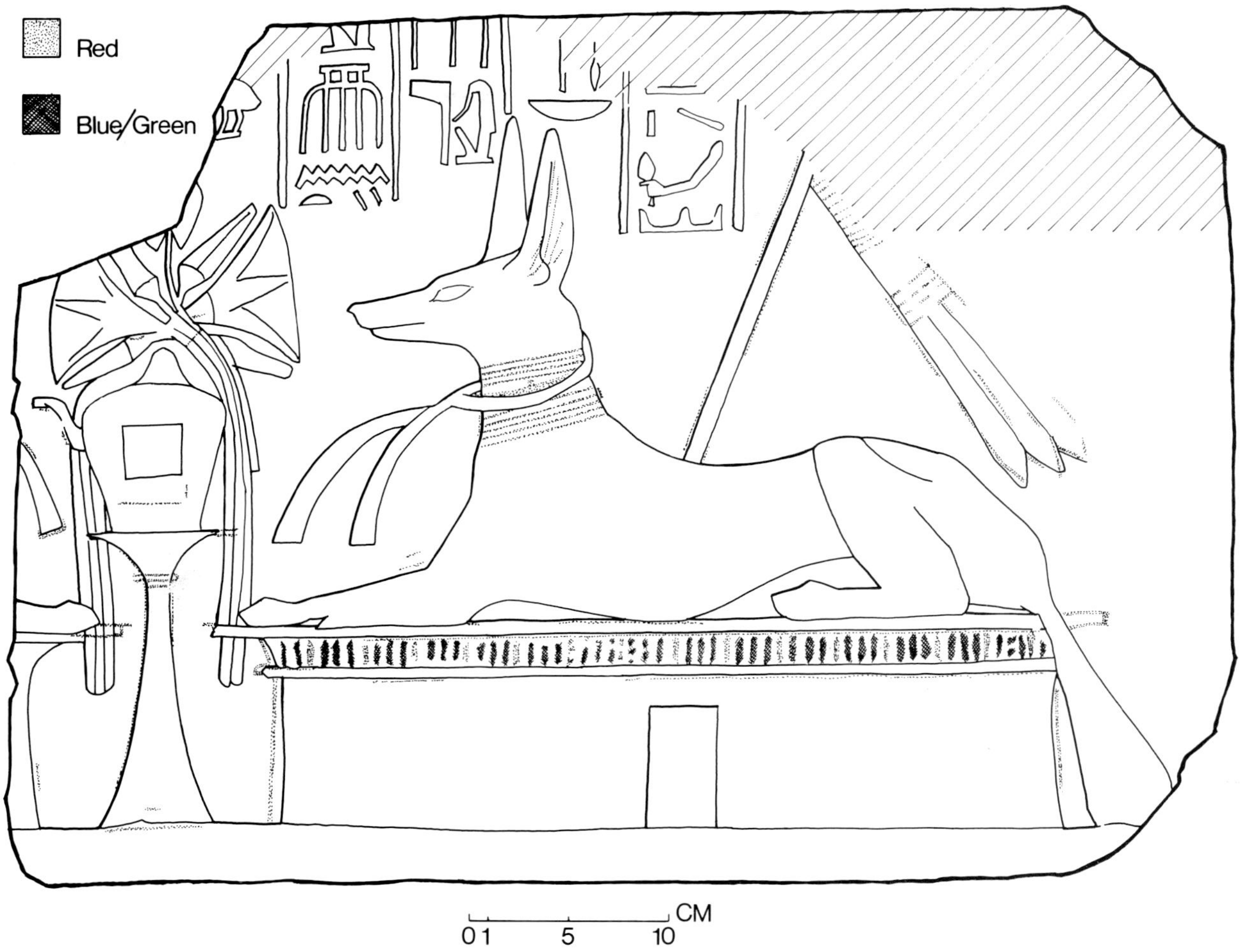

1. 455

2. 646

2. 700

1. 321

2.700

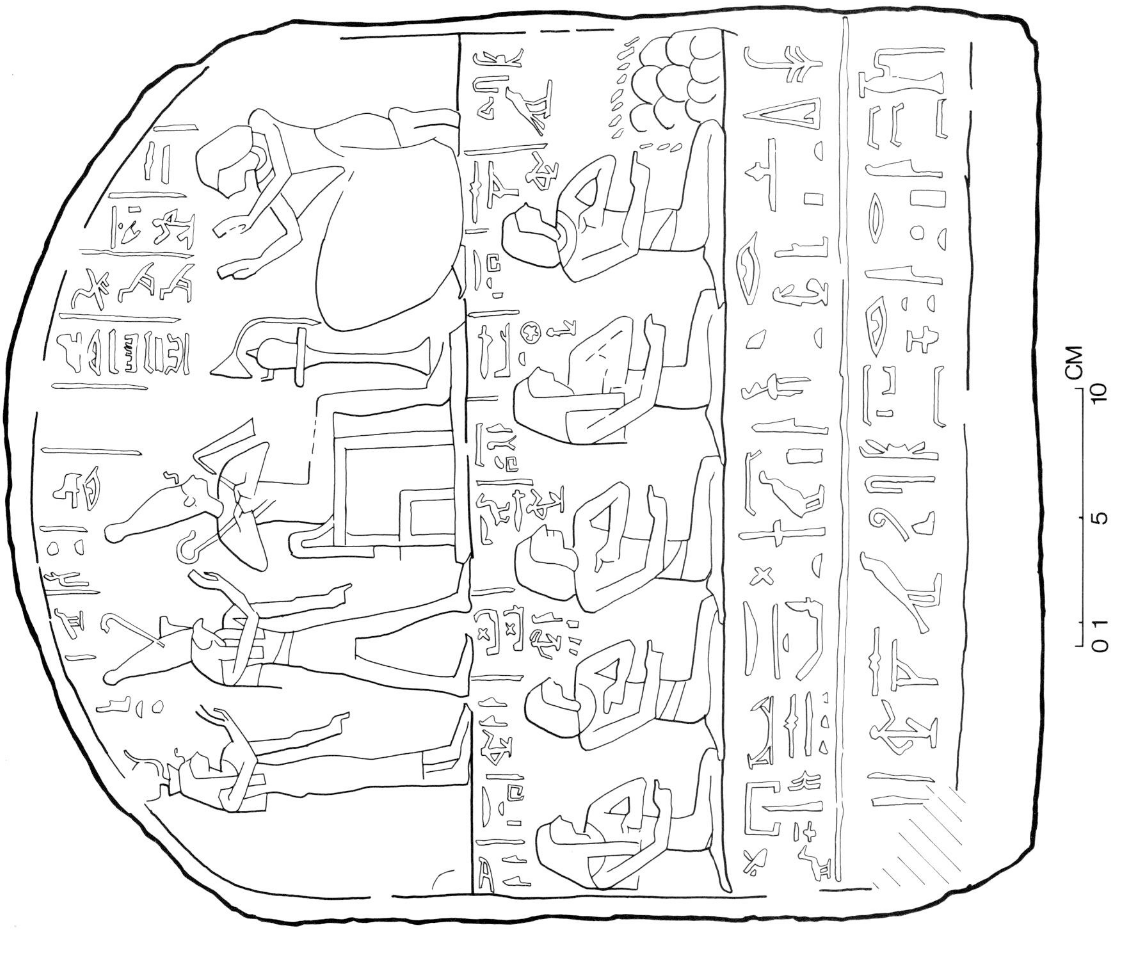

1.321

CM
0 1 5 10

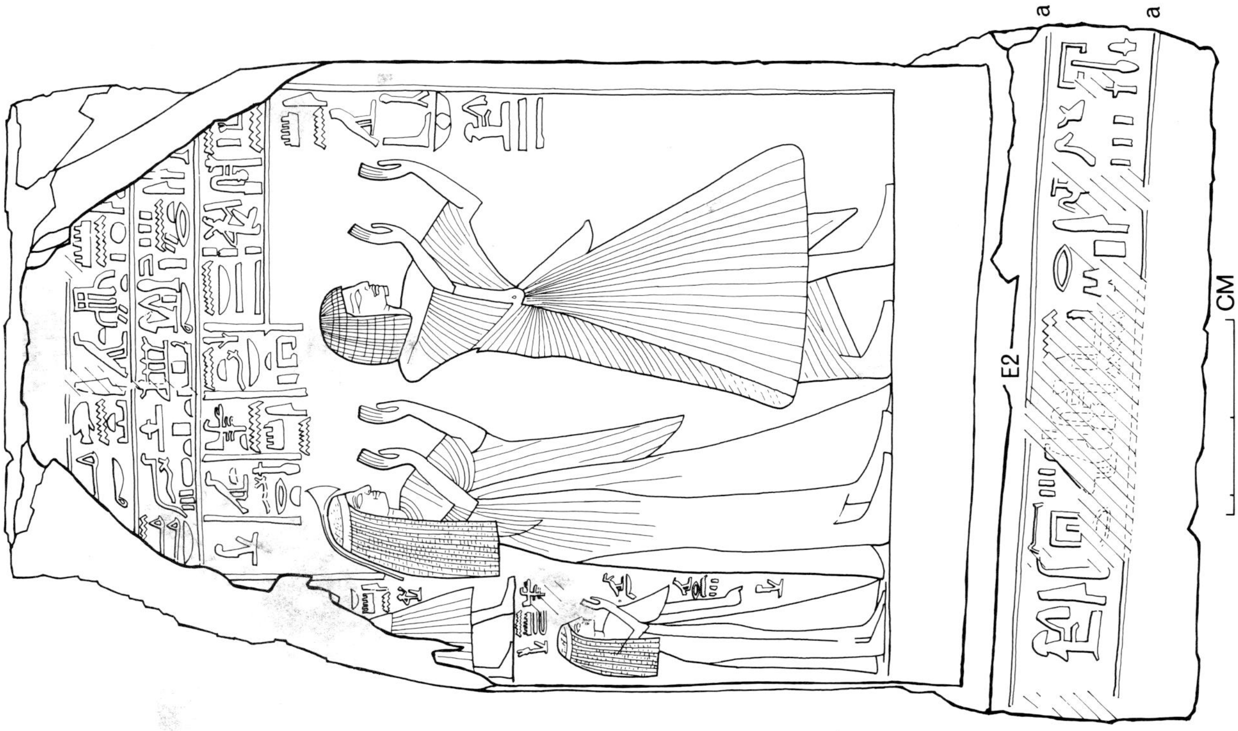

B

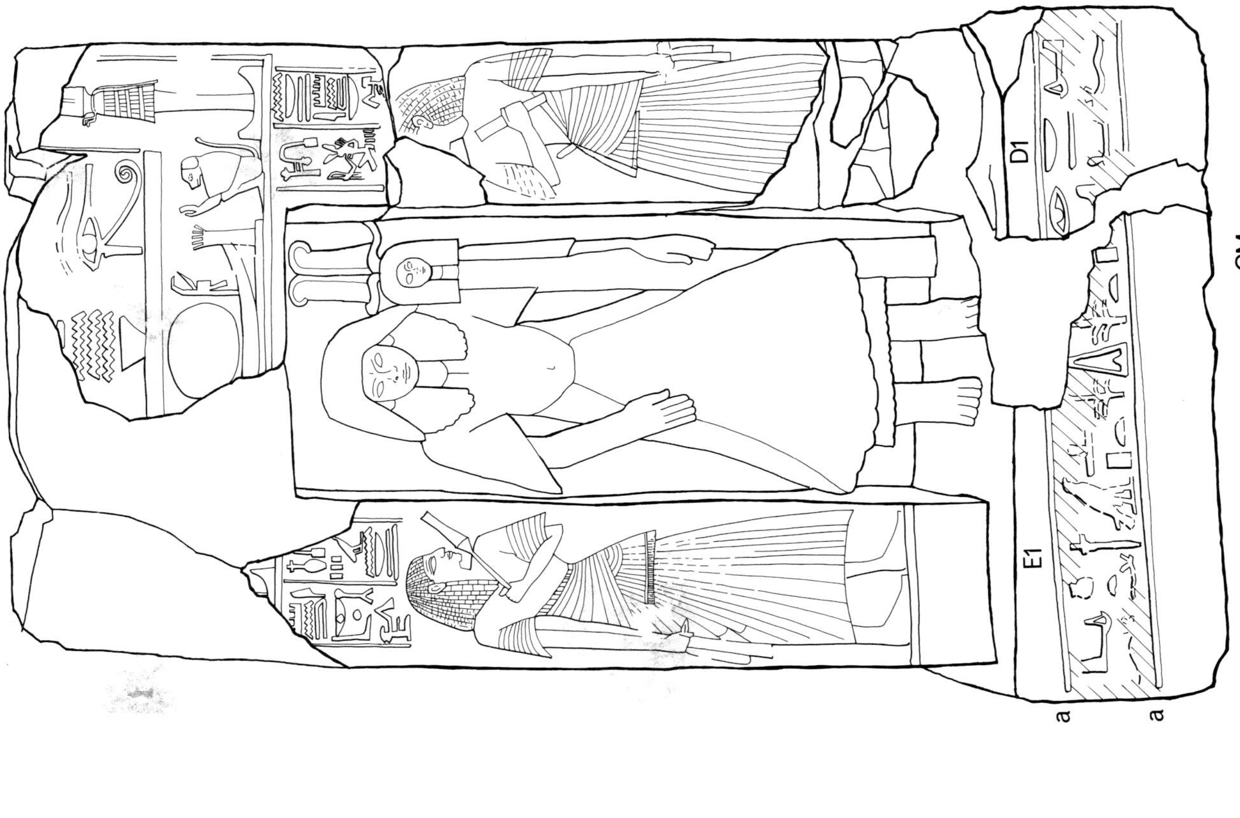

A

F

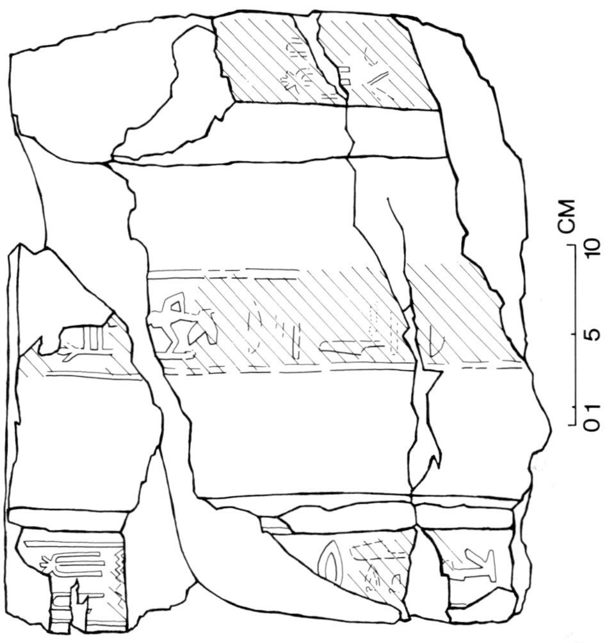

C

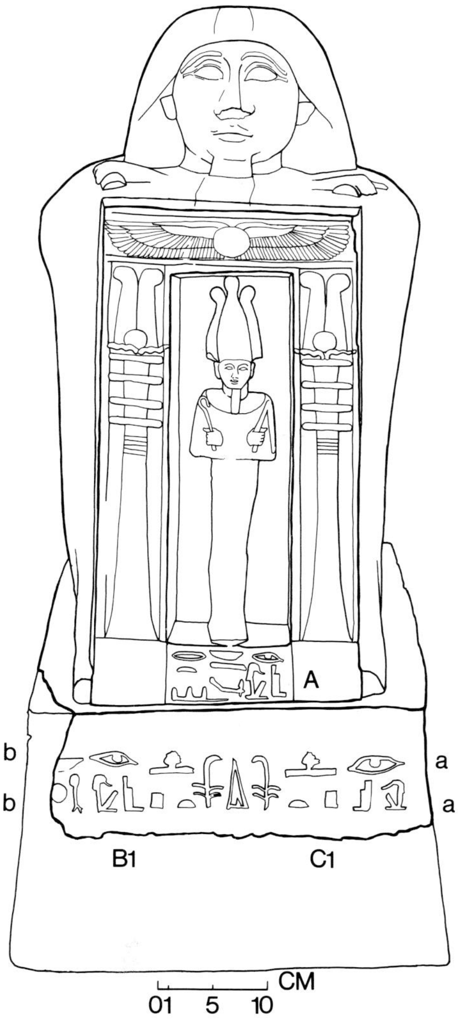
A
b
b
a
a
B1
C1
CM
01 5 10

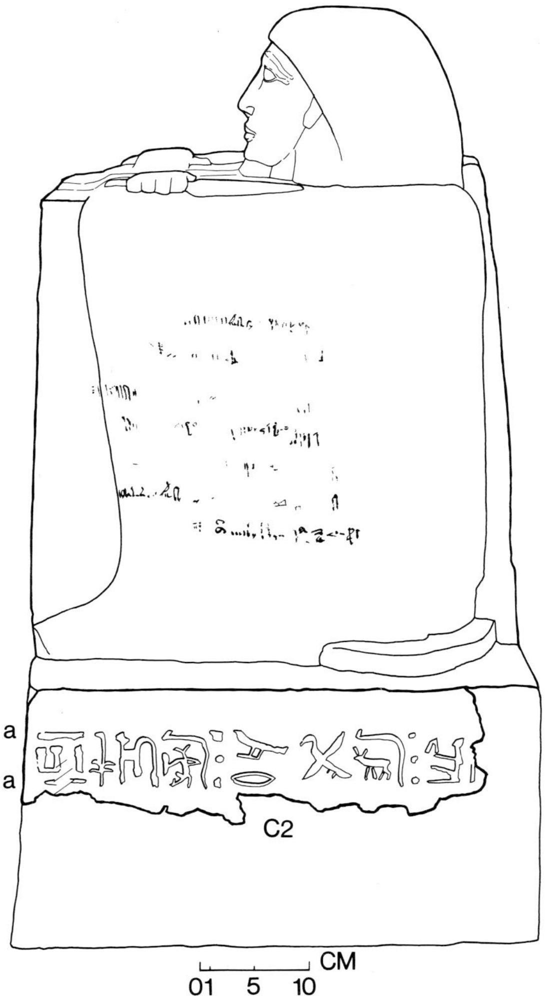
a
a
C2
CM
01 5 10

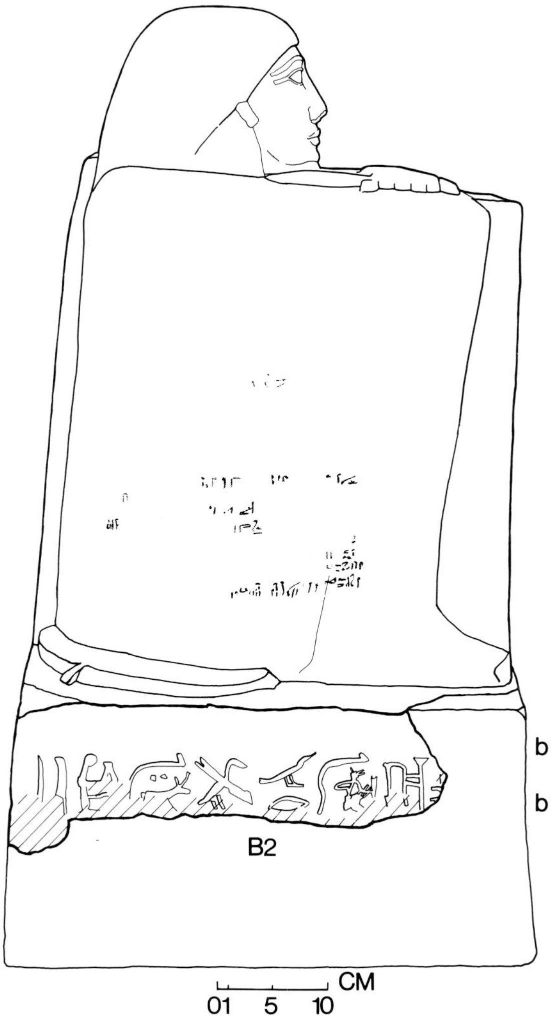
b
b
B2
CM
01 5 10

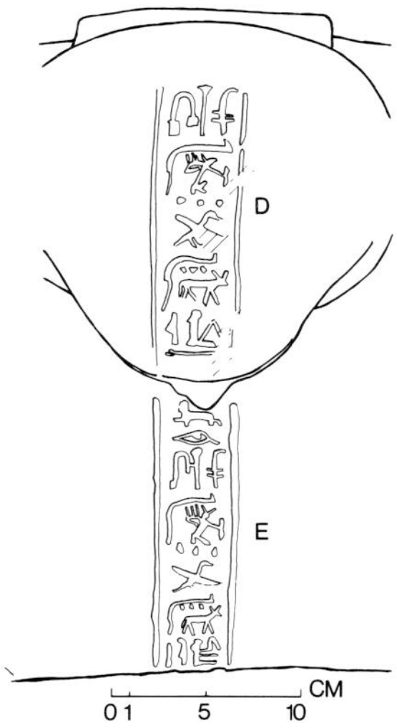
D
E
CM
0 1 5 10

2. 1430

1. 168

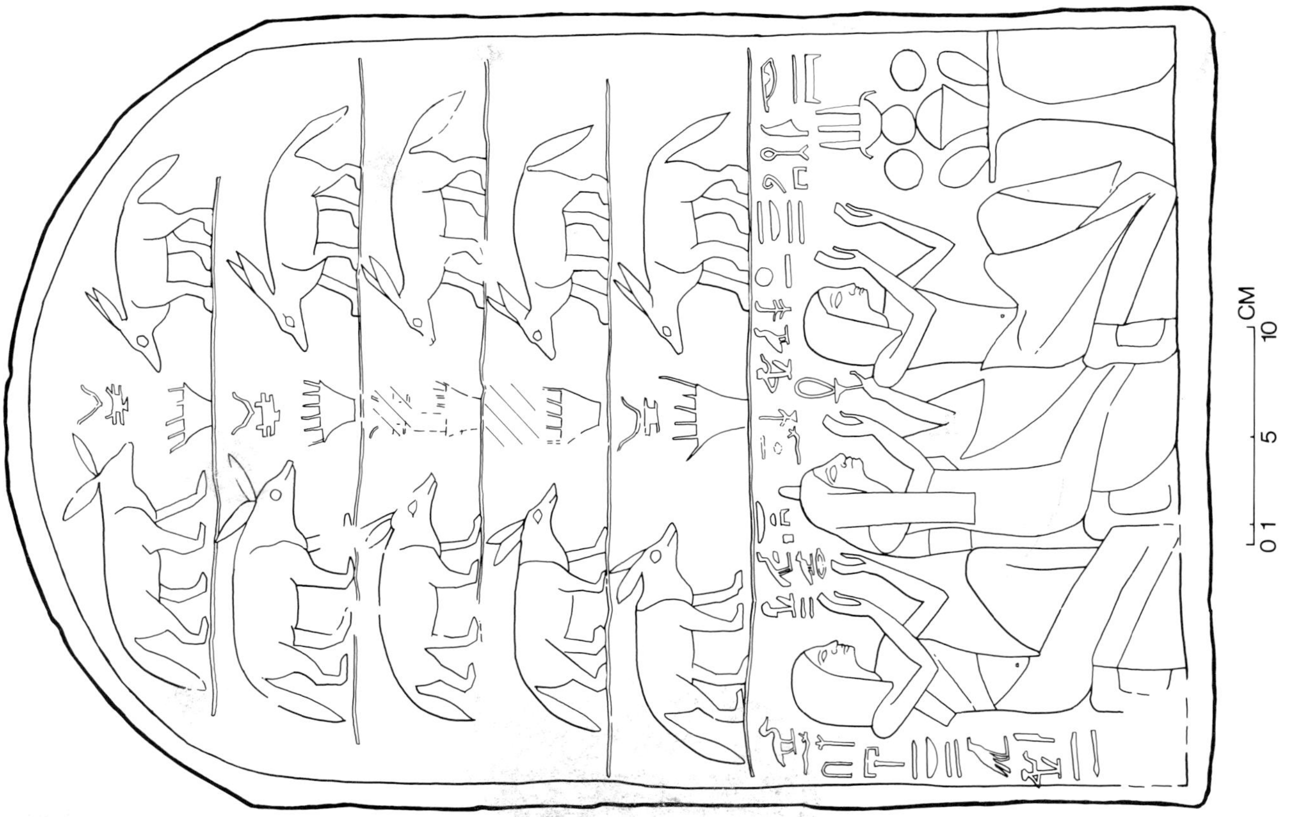

2. 1430

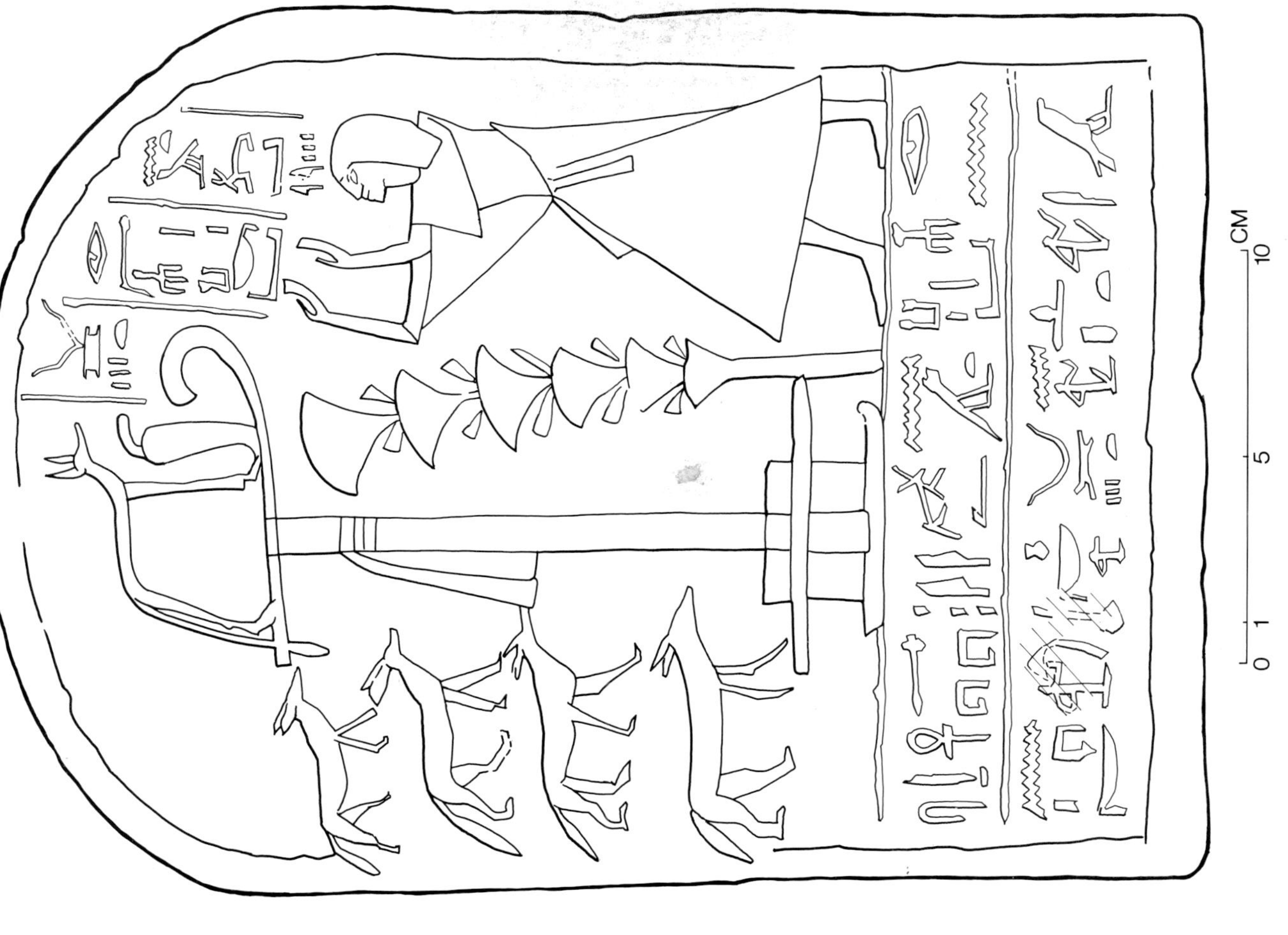

1. 891

2. 1725

1. 1632

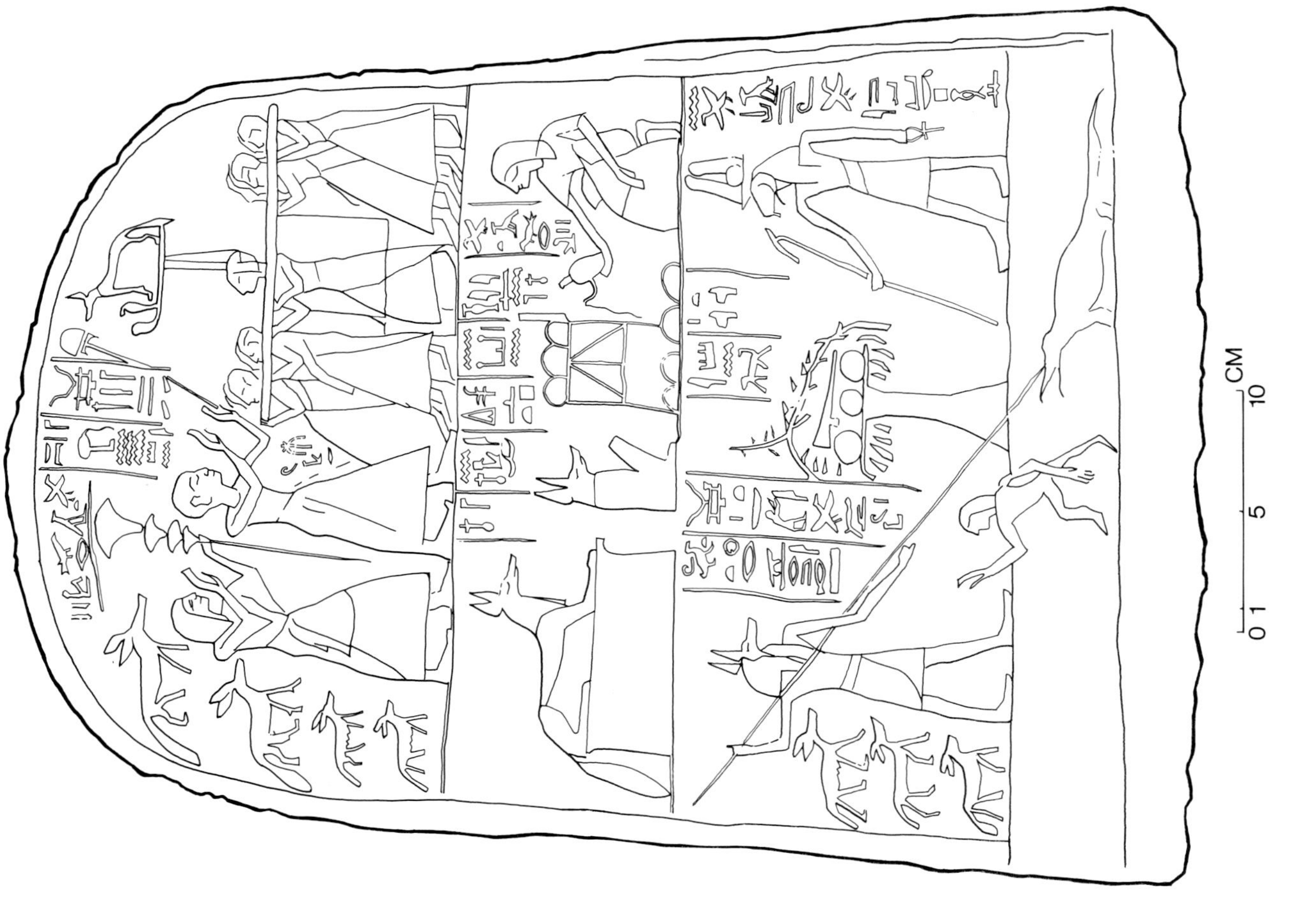

1. 1632

2. 1725

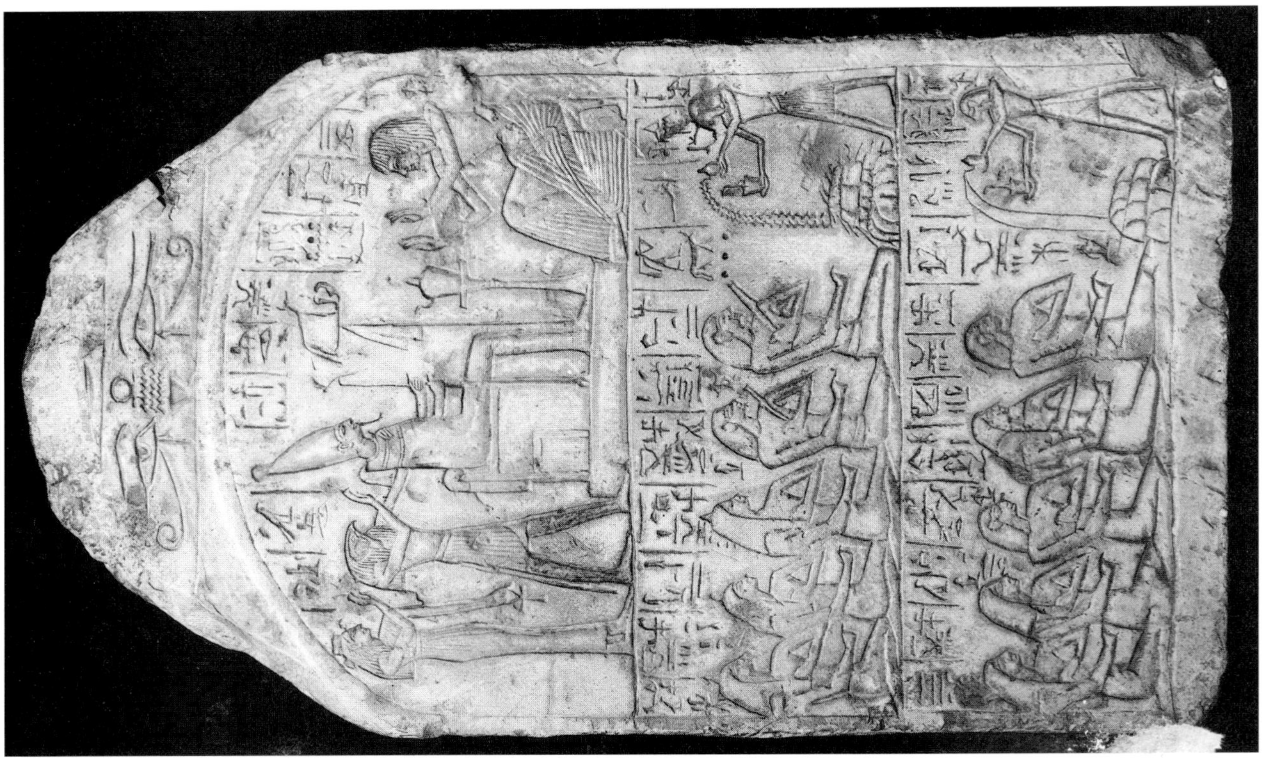

2. 1184

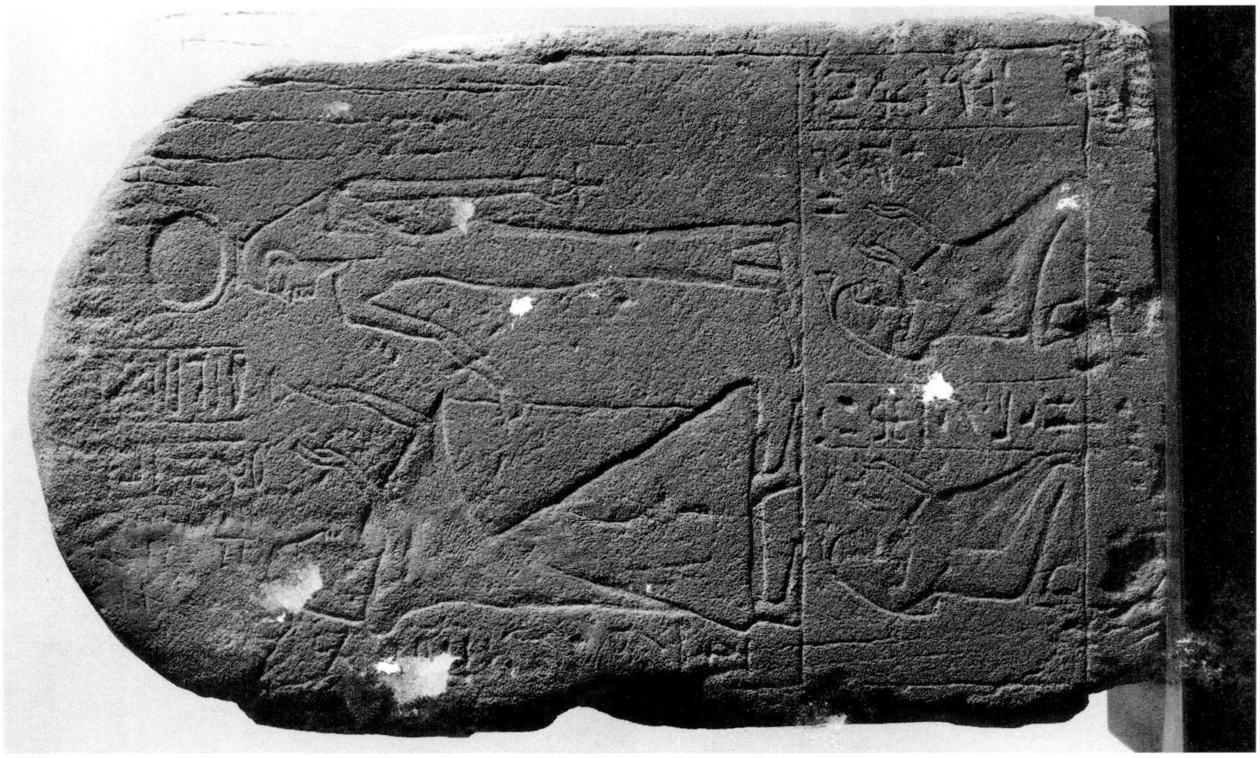

1. 1831

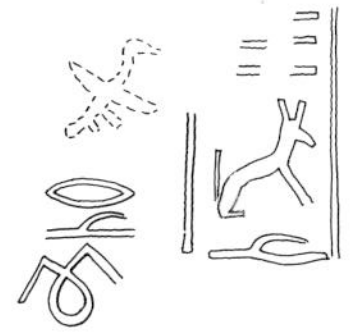

Traces recorded in earlier publication

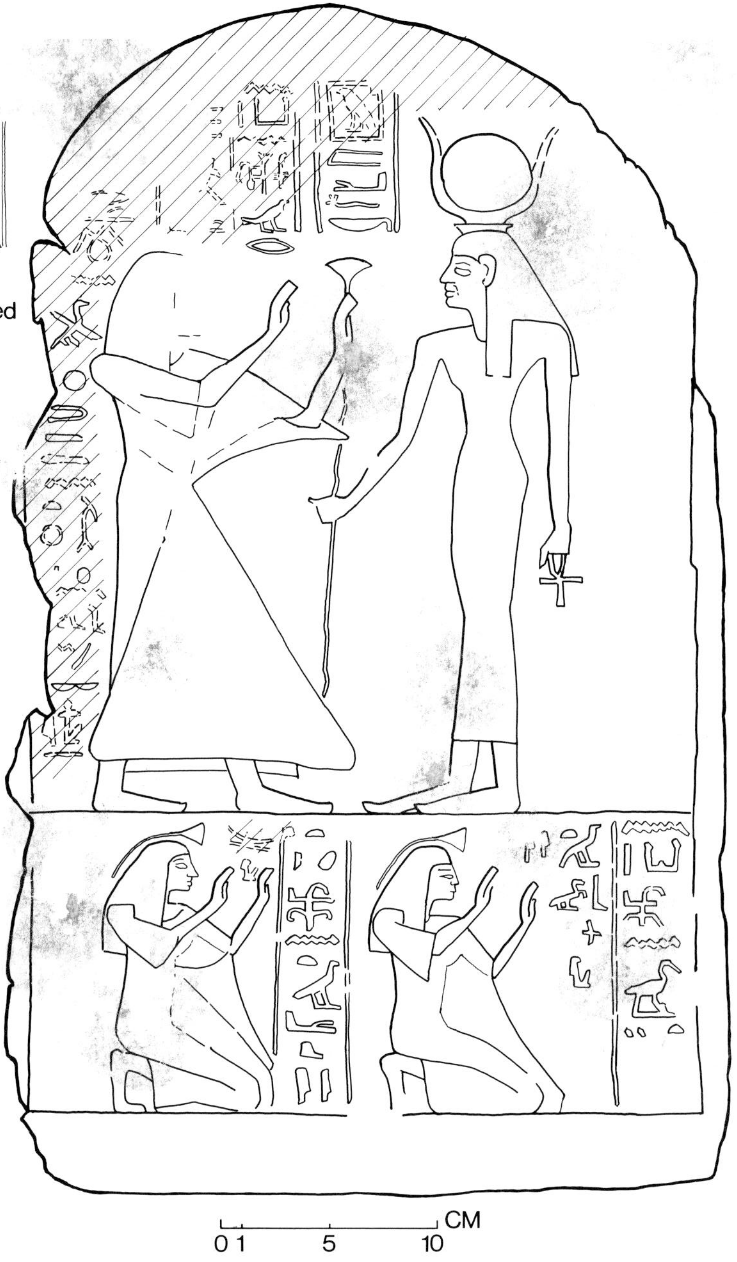

1. 1831

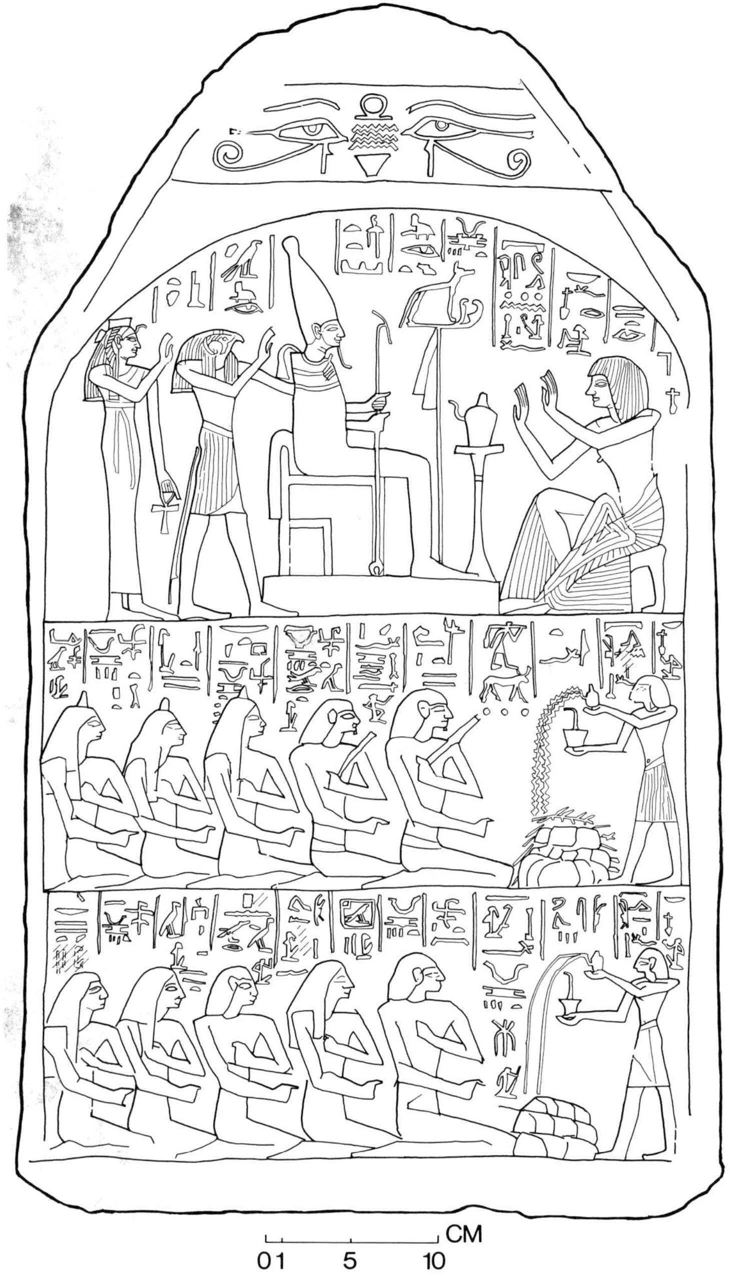

2. 1184

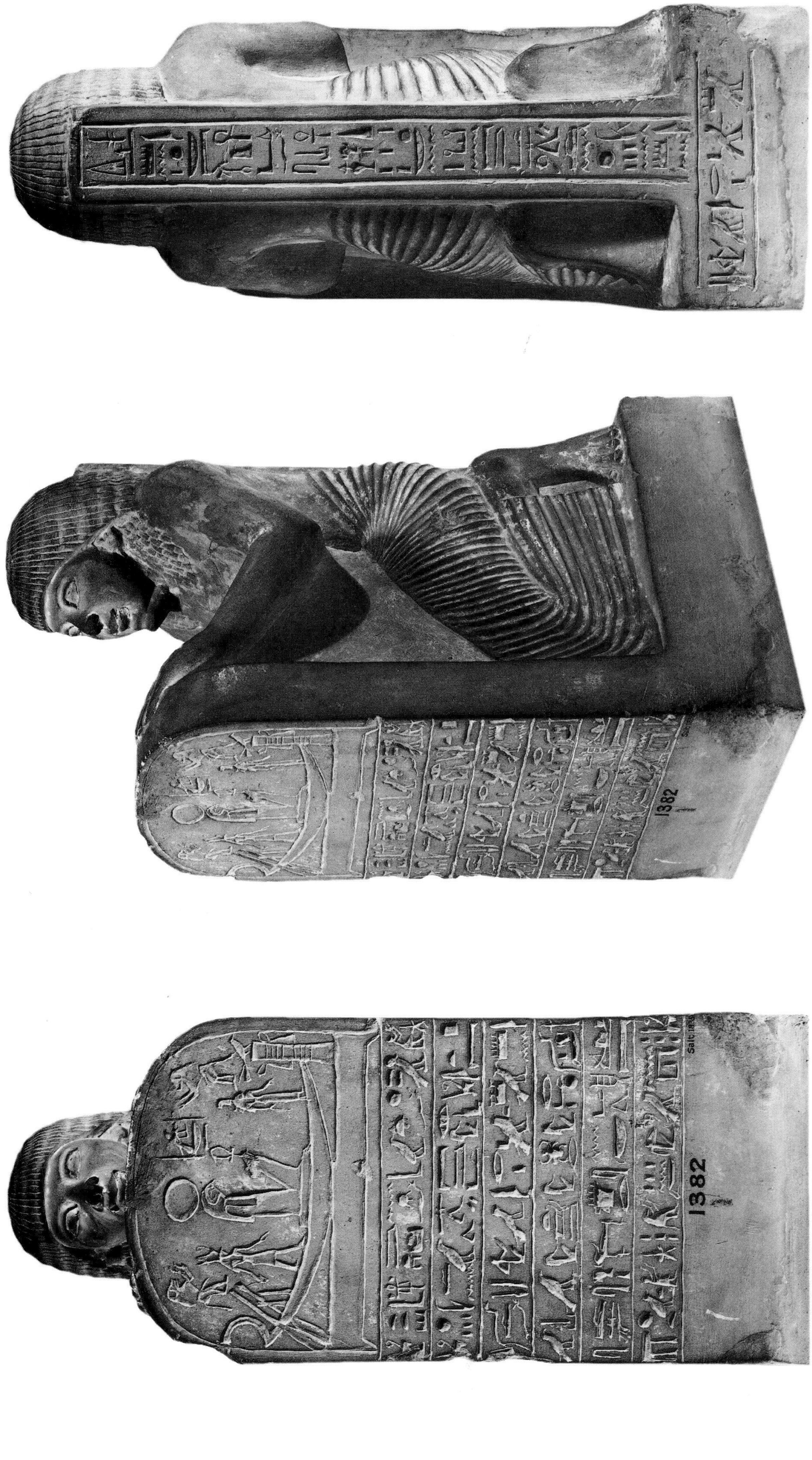

1382

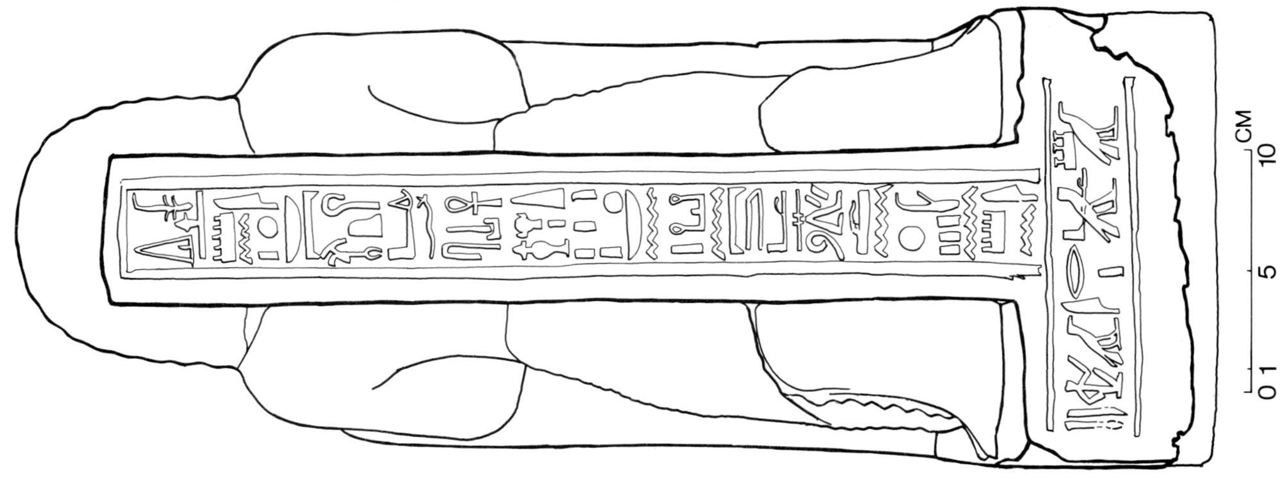

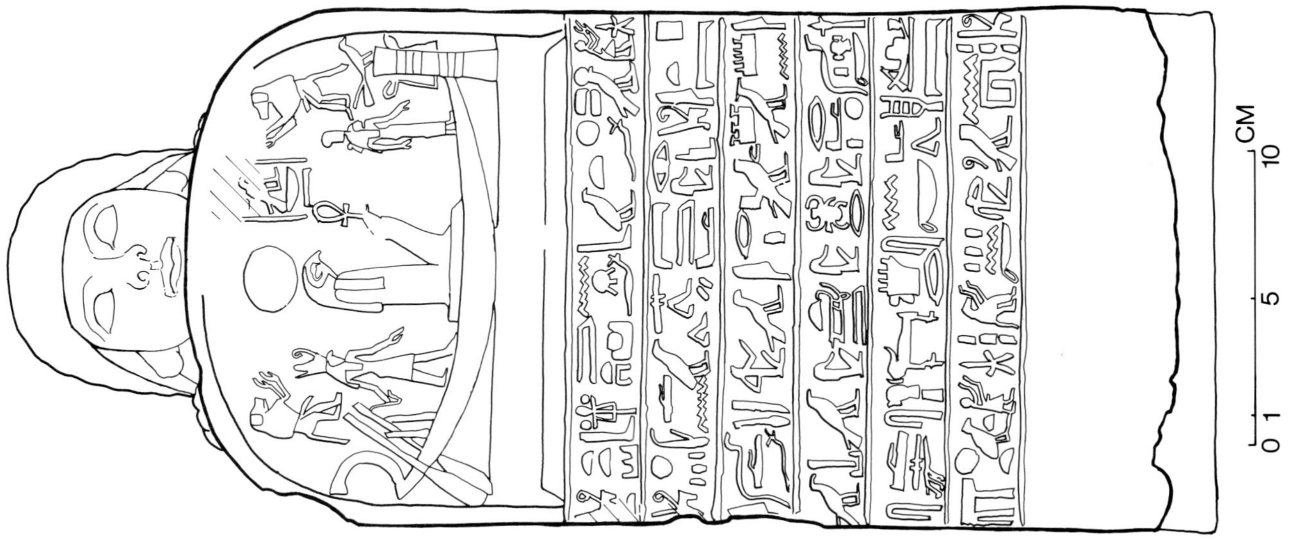

1382

1135

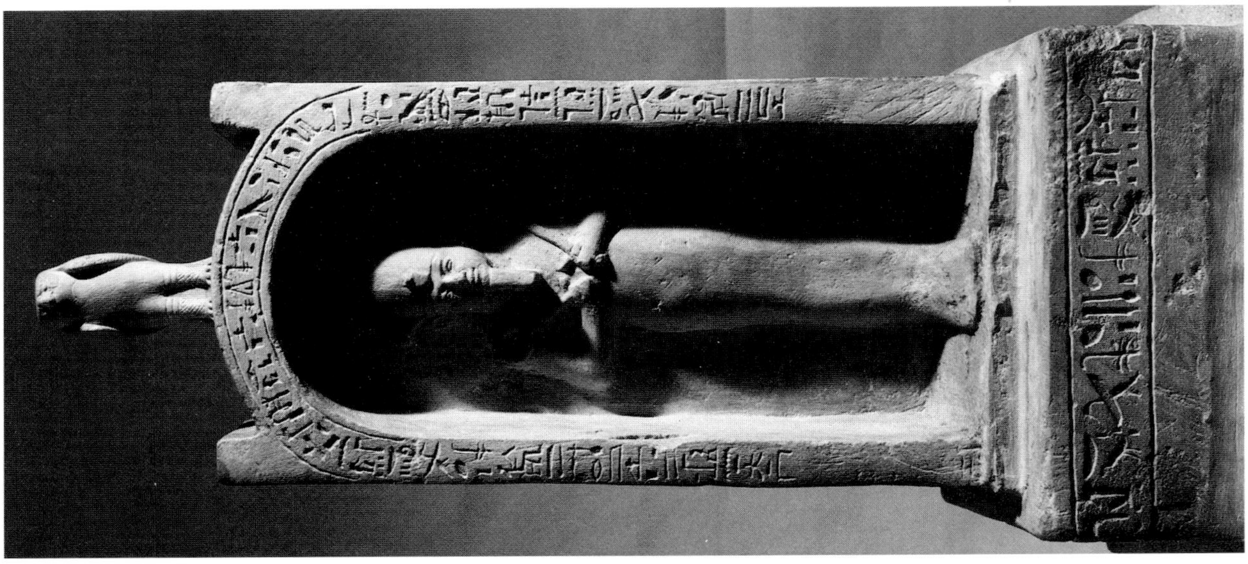

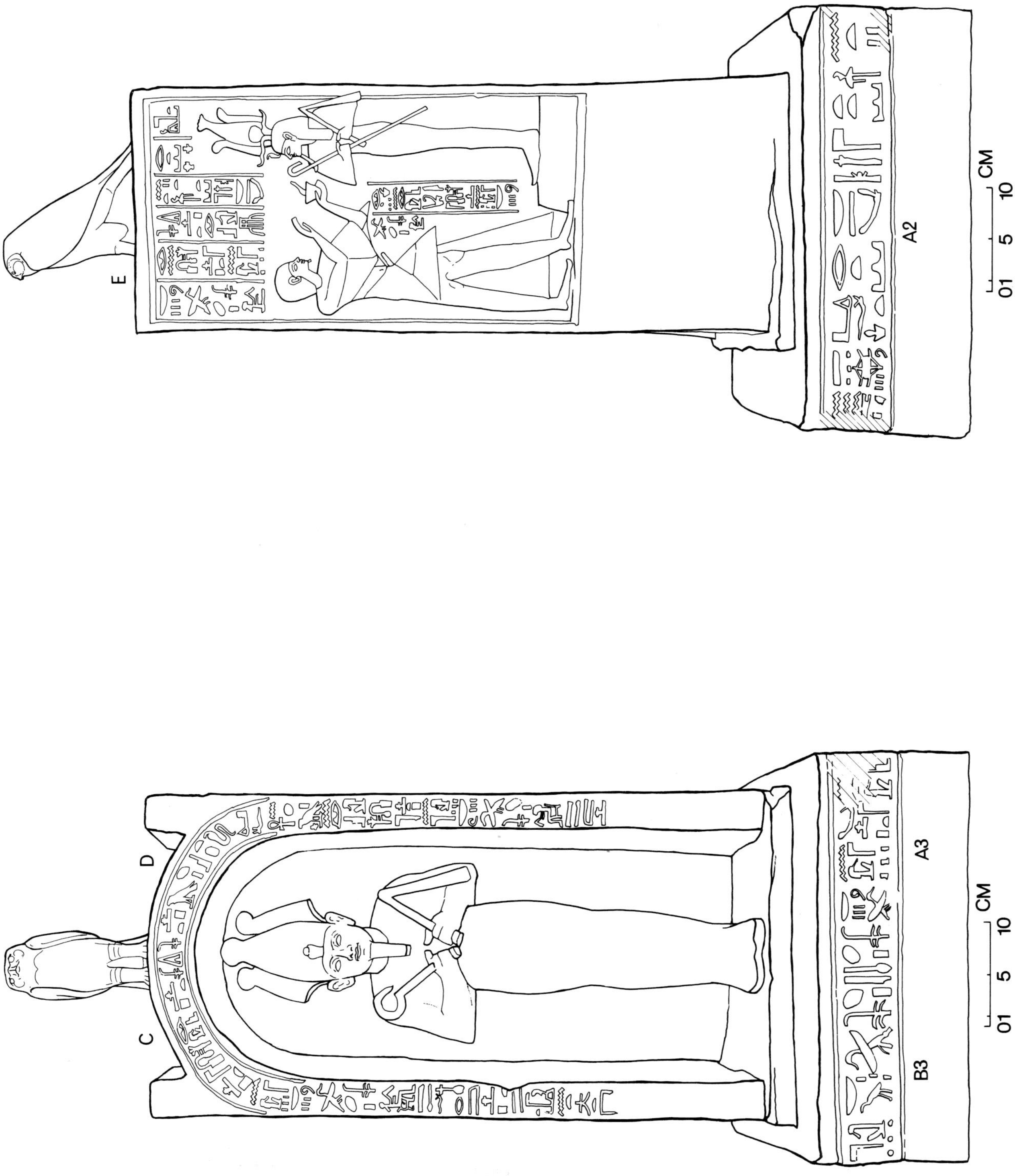

1135

PLATE 90

1135

G

H

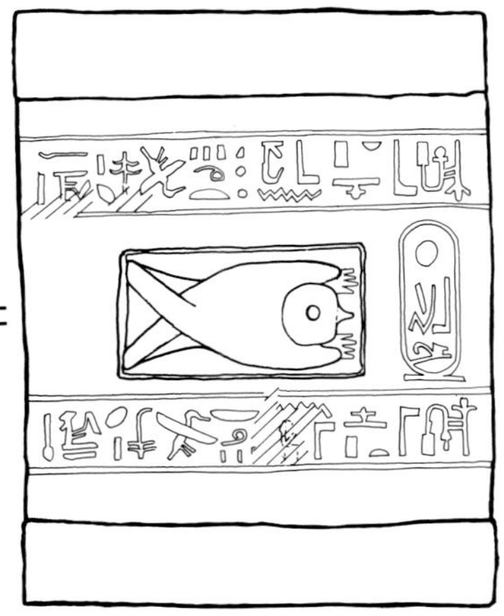

1135

F

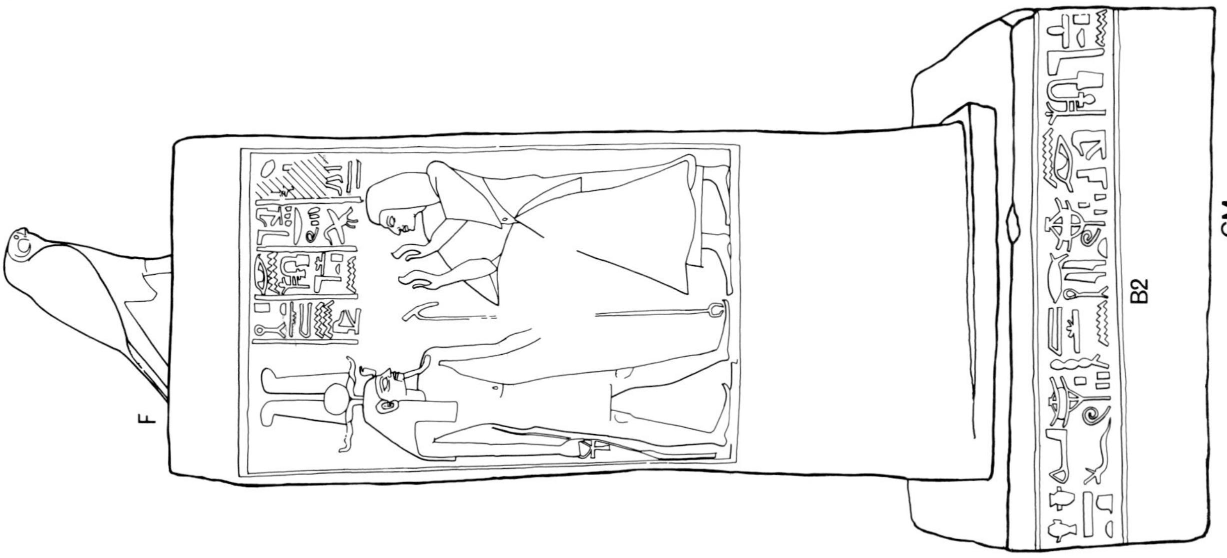

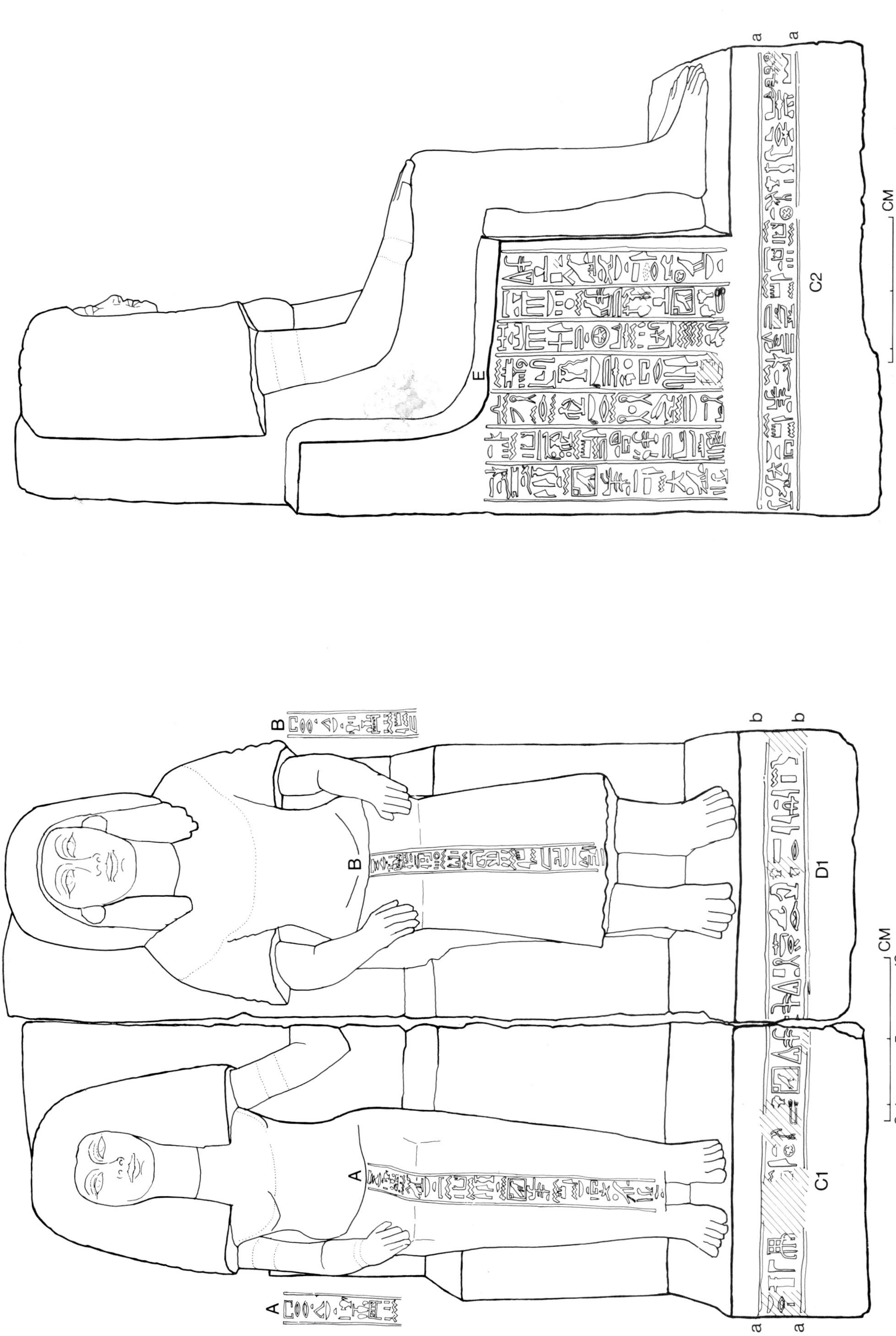
A
B
C1
C2
D1
E
a
b
0 1 5 10 CM

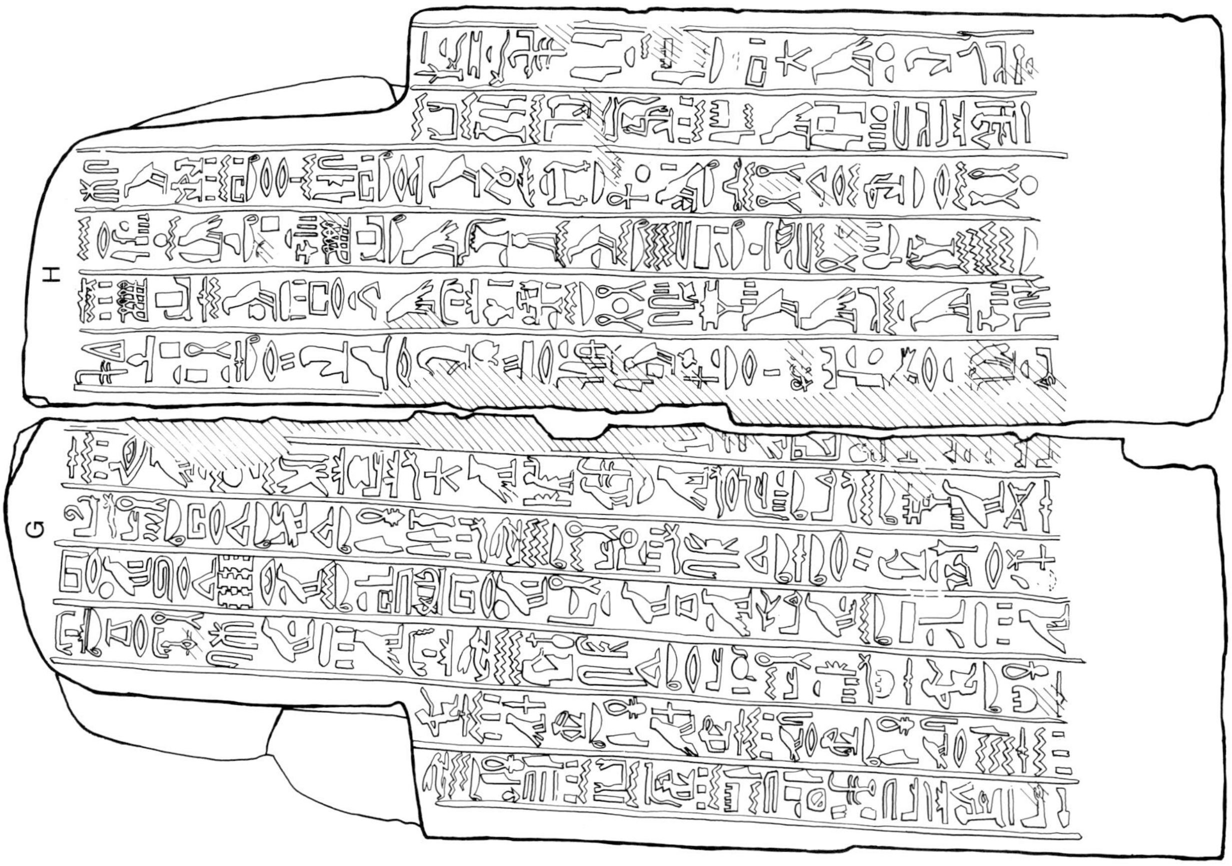
H
G
0 1 5 10 CM

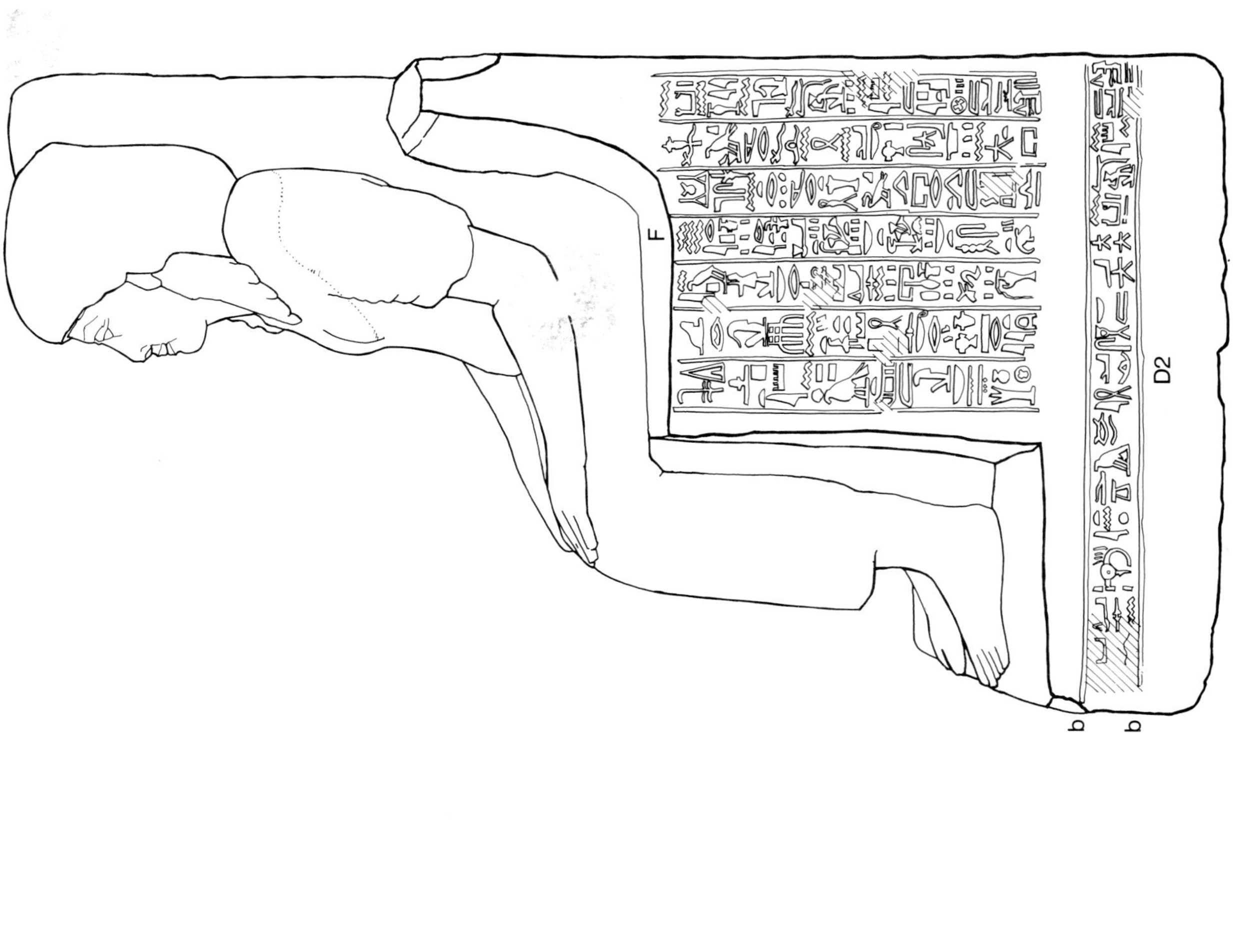
F
D2
0 1 5 10 CM
b
b

1. 484

2. 1753

3. 1471

1. 484

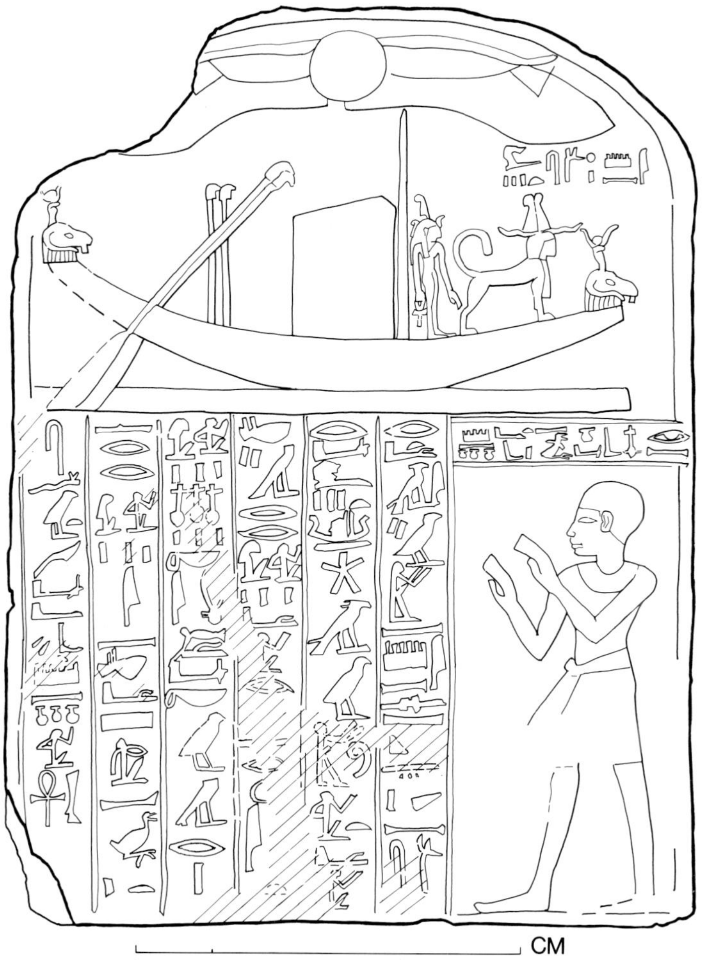

2. 1753

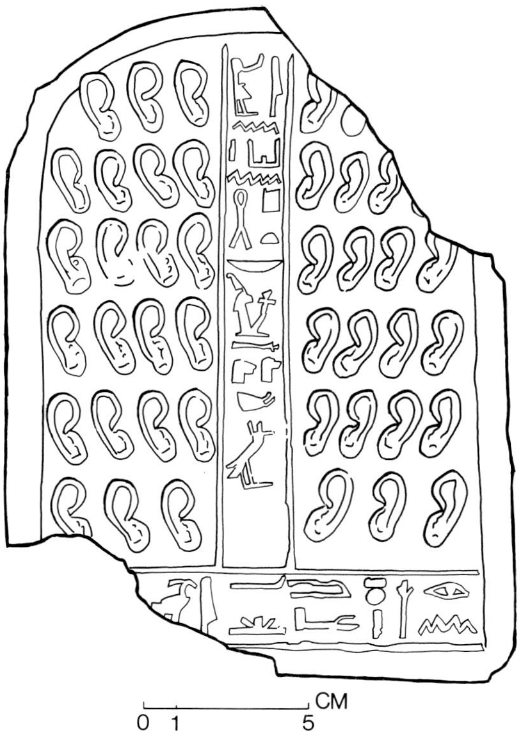

3. 1471

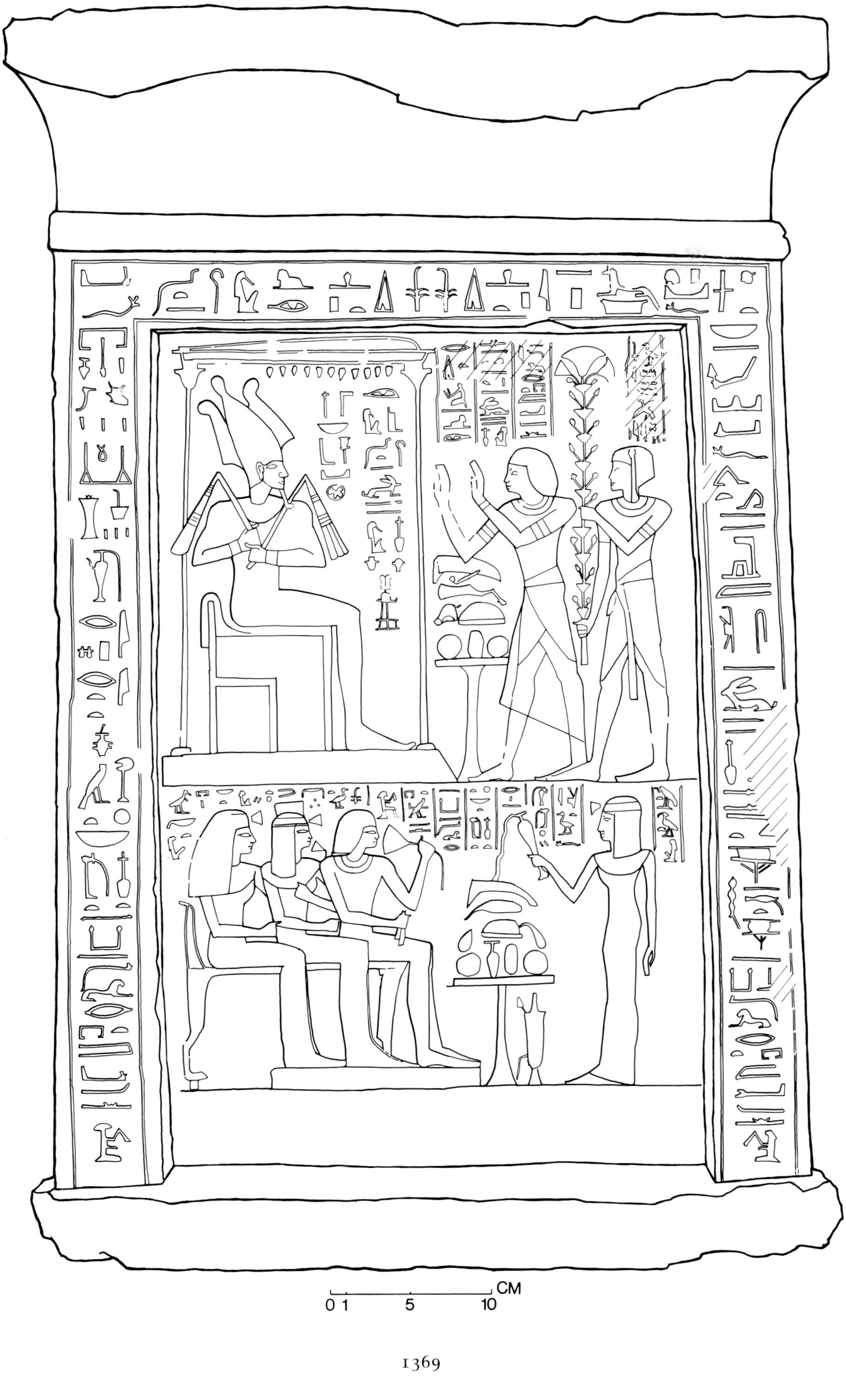

1369

2. 1745

1. 772

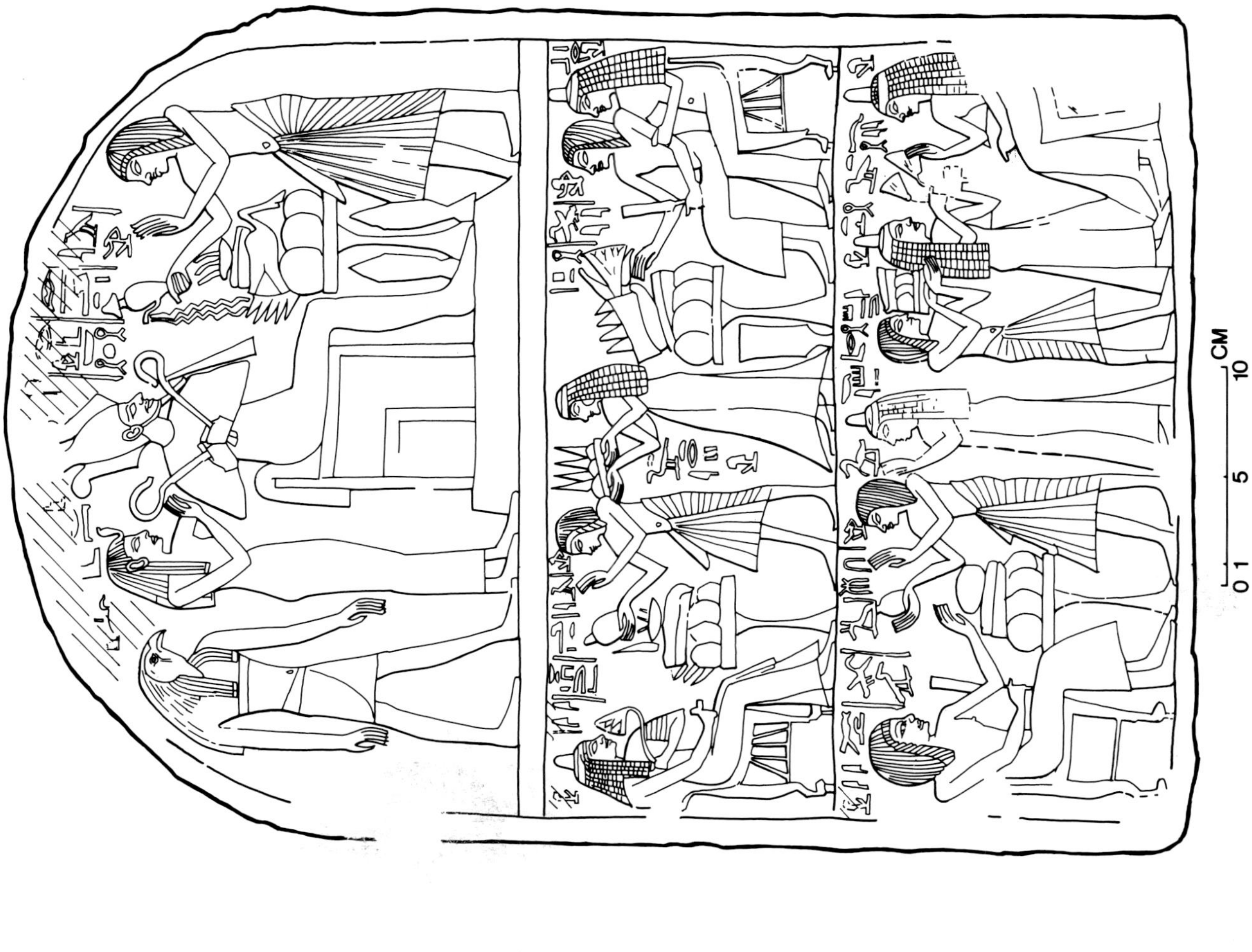

1. 772

2. 1745

2. 323

1. 364

2. 323

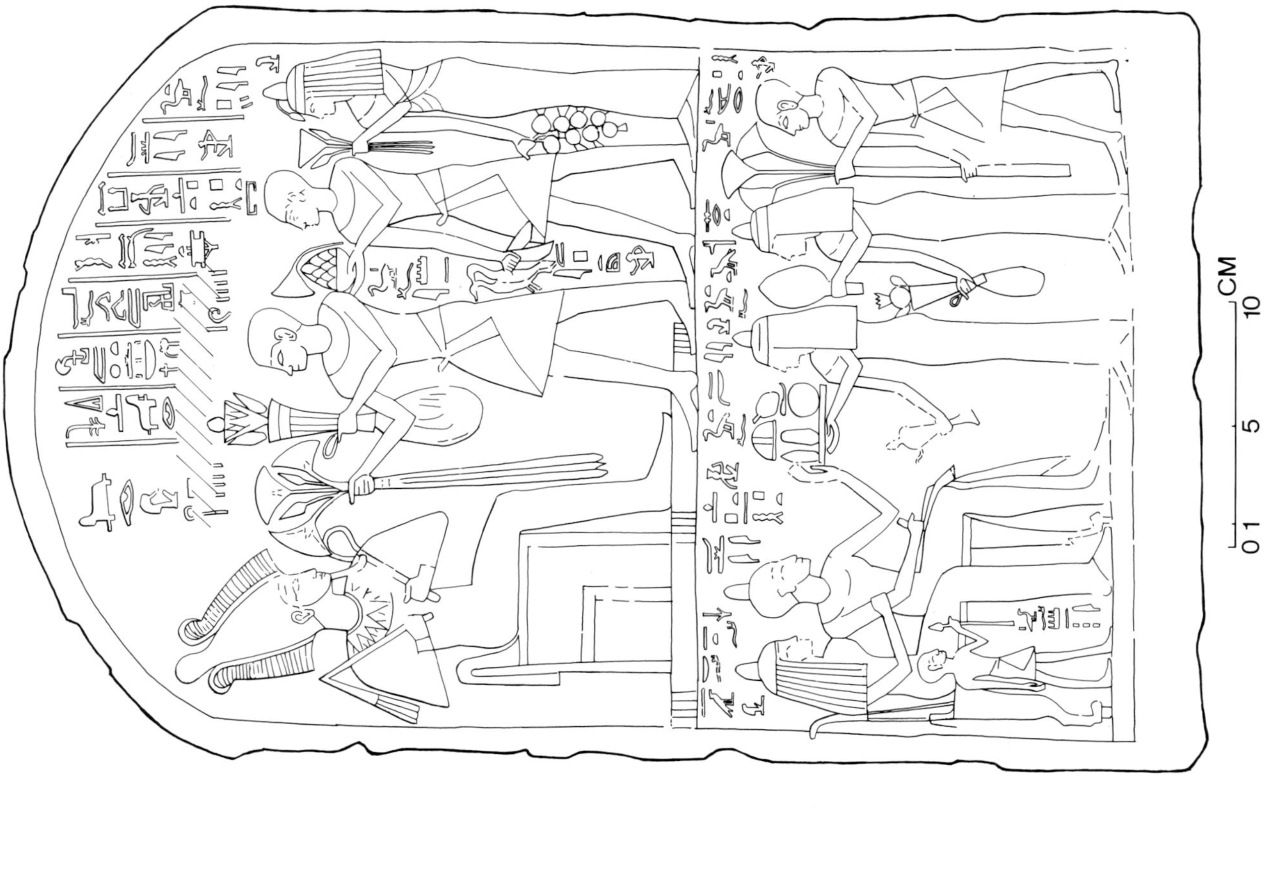

1. 364